**TOWN
MEMOIR**

D1490130

Salem

From Naumkeag to Witch City

town memoirs (toun mem´wärs). 1. True stories that capture the spirit of a community, its genius loci. 2. Anecdotes
passed on within a community from generation to generation.
3. A series of books by regional storytellers, illustrated by
local artists, preserving the popular history of great American
towns.

In the summer of 1909 Salem mayoral candidate Arthur Howard started his second Salem newspaper, the Gazette. *Now he could scream, in huge Hearstian headlines, that two of the three newspapers in Salem supported his candidacy for mayor.*

TOWN MEMOIRS

Salem

From Naumkeag to Witch City

[signature: Jim McAllister]

By Jim McAllister

Illustrated by Racket Shreve

[signature: Racket Shreve]

Commonwealth Editions

Beverly, Massachusetts

To My Parents, Bill and Alma

Designed by Janis Owens

Published and distributed by Commonwealth Editions,
an imprint of Memoirs Unlimited, Inc.,
21 Lothrop Street, Beverly, Massachusetts 01915.

Visit our website at commonwealtheditions.com.

Printed in the United States of America

Contents

Eighteenth Century

Nineteenth Century

Twentieth Century

Acknowledgments

Special thanks are due to Webster and Katie Bull of Commonwealth Editions for providing the opportunity to put these stories in print; to the *Salem Evening News* (within whose pages a number of these stories have appeared in one form or other); and to Racket Shreve for his wonderful illustrations. I am also deeply indebted to John Frayler and Peter LaChapelle at the Salem Maritime National Historic Site and to Bob Murphy at Higginson Books for reading and critiquing my manuscript.

In addition, I would like to take this opportunity to express my gratitude to the wonderful people of Salem and Essex County whose support has made it possible for me to continue doing what I love to do. A special thank-you goes out to the folks at the Hawthorne Hotel, the Lyceum Bar and Grill, the former Salem State College and Endicott College Elderhostel programs, and the Salem Chamber of Commerce.

The lengthy list of local businesses, organizations, and institutions to which I am indebted also includes the Salem Haunted Happenings Committee, the North Shore Medical Center, the Hamilton Hall Ladies Committee, the Salem Arts Lottery Council, and the Salem Five Cent Savings Bank. CAB Health and Recovery (formerly the Center for Addictive Behaviors), the now-defunct *Salem Pioneer*, the former Salem Witch Trials Tercentenary Committee, and Historic Salem, Inc., belong on this list, as do the City of Salem and dozens of area church groups, schools, historic societies, art associations, and fraternal groups.

Rounding out the list, as memory permits, are the Salem Trolley Corporation, the Salem Maritime National Historic Site and Visitor Center, the Peabody Essex Museum, the House of Seven Gables, and the Salem Witch Museum. Local newspapers, especially the *Salem Evening News*, the *Boston Globe*, and *North Shore Sunday*, have been far more generous to me than I probably deserve.

Finally, I extend my undying gratitude and endless affection to my wonderful family and to (in alphabetical order) Dave Arsenault, Steve Barnes, Anne Driscoll, Joan Gormalley and the "Chamberettes," Lee Hartmann, Tom MacLeod, JoAnn Souza, Joan Troy, Patti O'Hare Williams, Pete Zaharis, and others too numerous to mention. Without their ongoing support, encouragement, and friendship, I probably would have packed it in a long time ago.

—Jim McAllister
March 2000

Seventeenth Century

Although the Pickering House underwent periodic physical changes over the centuries, one thing stayed the same. For more than three hundred and fifty years, until the string was broken in the late 1990s, the house was inhabited by eleven generations of Pickerings, all of them direct descendants of the original John Pickering. No other house in America can match this record of continuous family occupancy.

Roger Conant comes to town

ల్)

On Washington Square in Salem, atop a massive boulder, stands a bronze statue of a man clothed in what is obviously seventeenth-century garb. Just over his left shoulder is the gothic, multi-turreted Salem Witch Museum. For obvious reasons many visitors assume the sculpted figure is a witch. One prestigious national magazine even called it a "determined sorceress."

But the man depicted in the statue is Roger Conant, who brought the first settlers to "Naumkeag" in the fall of 1626. The memorial sculpture was commissioned by the Conant Family Association in 1913 and is the work of Henry Kitson.

For Roger and his wife Sarah (Horton), Naumkeag was their fifth home in five years. The Conants had been living in London in 1622, but early the following year they set off for the New World in search of a better life. They landed at Plymouth, but as an outsider unwilling to participate fully in the society there, Roger was viewed by with suspicion by the plantation's elders. In 1624 he left that community to join others like himself in a settlement developing at Nantasket.

The Conants were just settling into their new life in Nantasket when Roger accepted an offer from the English Dorchester Company to take control of its two-year-old fishing plantation at Cape Ann. He and his family spent part of 1625 and most of 1626 at Cape Ann before they and the remaining settlers there relocated to Naumkeag when the Dorchester Company gave up on the Cape Ann settlement.

Roger Conant and his growing family were tired of moving. When some of the other Naumkeag settlers moved to warmer climates following the first brutal winter, the Conants decided to stay. They stayed despite having to live in a cramped, dirt-floored dugout carved into the banks of the North River. They stayed even though the help promised by Dorchester Company founder John White failed to arrive.

The Conants probably contemplated leaving Naumkeag when John Endicott arrived to take control of the plantation in 1628. As the legal representative of the New England Company, which had acquired the property and the rights of the defunct Dorchester Company, Endicott replaced Conant as the leader of the settlement. But again Conant decided to stay and help make Naumkeag work. He cooperated with Endicott and the other new settlers, and that cooperation earned the community a new name: Salem, city of peace.

It was certainly to the benefit of the community that Conant did stay. He served in many official posts, including selectman and representative to the General Court, and was a valued member of the community until his death in 1679.

The Conants, incidentally, moved once more, across the river to the Bass River Side section of town. In the 1660s, Bass River Side separated from Salem and became what is now Beverly.

The passing of the Naumkeags

ℰℐ

Part of the appeal of Naumkeag for Conant and his followers was that the local Native Americans offered the use of cleared lands for growing crops. The Naumkeag tribe no longer needed the land. Its population had been greatly reduced in the decade preceding Conant's arrival.

In 1616 a comet had crossed the horizon, a sign to the Naumkeags that "some strange thing would follow." The next summer, a "sore consumption" descended on the tribe. This plague, probably introduced by European fishermen and explorers, lasted for three years and claimed the lives of approximately 90 percent of the Native Americans living along the New England coast.

Organizing a church

୧/୬

Salem's First Church, currently located at 316 Essex Street, has the distinction of being the first Protestant church formed in America.

In 1629 approximately two hundred people, many of them Puritans fleeing religious persecution in England, landed in Salem. Among them were a number of ministers with a mandate from the Puritan-dominated Massachusetts Bay Company to establish a church.

Governor John Endicott had already determined that the church would adopt the form used by the Pilgrims in Plymouth; that is, it would be autonomous, answerable to its members rather than to a higher temporal authority. This was a first step toward separation from the hierarchical Church of England.

Two of the new arrivals to Salem, John and Samuel Browne, objected to the new church structure. The brothers invited others to join them in continuing to worship according to the Book of Common Prayer used in the Church of England liturgy. The Brownes quickly found themselves on a vessel heading back to England. Religious freedom, it was clear to all, would not be a hallmark of the new "Bible Commonwealth."

John Endicott gets in trouble

❧

One of the basic antipathies of the Puritans was to the Catholic Church, which they felt had corrupted the Church of England. The Catholic hierarchical structure, its holidays, and its teachings were all looked upon with disfavor. Even the names of the days and months on the Roman calendar were discarded in favor of numbers.

The British flag at this time featured a cross in the upper left-hand corner. To John Endicott and many other Puritans that cross smacked of the hated papacy and all it stood for.

One spring day in 1634 Endicott stood in Town House Square reviewing the local militia with the radical minister of the First Church, Roger Williams. When he spotted the flag with its hated cross, Endicott summoned the bearer to his side. Taking his sword from his scabbard, he removed the offending symbol from the ensign.

Many members of the Puritan power structure supported John Endicott's action privately. But they knew they had to punish him for defacing the King's flag or run the risk that the monarch would take action against the colony for what could be perceived as an act of treason. The General Court banned Endicott from holding office for a year.

Early sickness and death

❧

Early settlers in Salem suffered great hardships adjusting to life in the New World. They had to cope with radical changes in diet, a lack of decent shelter, and the onslaught of germs against which their bodies had yet to build up immunity. Great sicknesses claimed many lives in the winters of 1628 and 1629.

Being governor of the colony offered one little protection against disease or other cruelties of life. One of the first to die after the arrival of Governor John Endicott's party was the governor's own beloved wife. Endicott's successor was John Winthrop, who arrived in June of 1630 in the *Arbella*. With Winthrop came eleven other vessels and approximately 1,100 new settlers. The new arrivals stayed in Salem only a few weeks before the lack of food, water, and shelter prompted them to move on to Charlestown and eventually to Boston.

John Winthrop's first letter home to his wife contained sad tidings. The day after his arrival their twenty-two-year-old son Henry attempted to swim across the North River to see the Indian encampment in the North Fields. Just a few rods from the shore he got a cramp and drowned.

A tale of two ministers

ભ

Roger Williams was a problem.

Williams, the former assistant to the Reverend Samuel Skelton, had been elected minister of Salem's First Church in 1634 after Skelton's death. The colonial authorities were upset about his selection. They had already seen and heard enough of the radical and outspoken man of the cloth.

Some of Williams's publicized views ran contrary to those of the Puritan society, and others were bound to offend the monarchy and place the Massachusetts charter in jeopardy. Williams claimed the King had no right to give away the Native Americans' land and that church and state should be separate. He also insisted that there should be no contact whatsoever between the Puritans and the hated Church of England.

Efforts to silence Williams had elicited apologies and promises to change his ways. But those promises were short-lived. Finally, in 1635, the General Court voted to banish the troublesome cleric. Before he could be arrested and shipped back to England, Roger Williams escaped to the Plymouth Colony. There the ill minister was nursed backed to health by local Indians who also gave him the land that became Rhode Island.

Hugh Peter replaced Williams as minister of Salem's First Church. Peter tightened up the church covenant and rules and slowly began healing the rift between Williams's supporters and foes. Peter was also a boon to the town economy. During his time in Salem he organized the fisheries and raised capital both in the New World and abroad for fishing and shipbuilding. He encouraged the production of salt for preserving fish and the construction of a 300-ton fishing vessel. Within a year of his arrival, the settlement's first load of salted cod left for the West Indies.

Peter provided spiritual and economic leadership to the town until 1642, when he was selected to return to England to protect the colony's interests. There he served as chaplain and military leader under the leader of the successful Puritan rebellion, Oliver Cromwell. Peter's fortunes soared under Cromwell's administration, but he would pay the ultimate price when the monarchy was restored in 1660. The former Salem minister was arrested, hanged until almost dead, and disemboweled.

First school

❧

The town's first school was opened by John Fiske in 1637 and has been in operation, in one form or other, since that time. It is one of America's oldest public schools.

Fiske's was a "free" grammar school. Parents who could afford to do so paid what they could for their sons' tuition, and the town subsidized the rest. Salem's present public school system, which provides free education to all Salem children, dates to 1768.

Some of the funding for these early schools and schoolmasters came from the fees received each year from the operators of the ferries between Salem and the neighboring towns of Beverly and Marblehead. The income generated from the leasing of Baker's and Misery Islands was also applied to public schools.

A near miss

In 1635 Thomas Scruggs of Salem offered a 300-acre tract of land between Legg's Hill on the present-day Salem–Marblehead line and the ocean to the colony as a site for a college. But another location was ultimately chosen, and today Cambridge, not Salem, is the site of Harvard University.

Early transportation

Salem's first ferry was licensed by the town on December 26, 1636. John Stone was authorized to operate a boat between his home on the North River and Bass River Side (now Beverly) for a period of three years. The passage cost strangers two pennies, local residents only one.

William Dixey won the ferry contract in 1639 and was granted permission to transport animals as well as humans. Fees were set at six pennies for horses, cows, and "other great beasts" and two pennies for goats, swine, and calves. Tolls for all passengers doubled after dark.

The Salem–Marblehead ferry began operating in 1637 under a lease arrangement with George Wright. In 1717 a docking facility was built next to John Turner's wharf. This dock served as the new Salem terminus for the Marblehead ferry. The ticket office was supposedly located in what is now Hepzibah's shop in the House of Seven Gables. A third ferry shuttled passengers across the North River to Salem's North Fields. It ceased operation when the North Bridge was built in 1744, if not before.

The ferries generated headaches as well as income. In 1649 laws had to be passed allowing ferrymen to collect fares in advance of the trip (too many passengers were disembarking without paying) and to refuse unstrung wampumpeag offered as payment.

Passengers had their own complaints. Unsecured cargo and carriages sometimes slid off the ferries into the water and ferry employees frequently stopped mid-journey to help offload other vessels anchored in the harbor. This work brought the ferrymen extra income but caused their passengers "vexatious delay."

The Pickering House

In 1651 a carpenter named John Pickering built a two-room, two-story house on his farm on present-day Broad Street. Little did he know that his modest dwelling would one day achieve a distinction that no other house in America could match.

John Pickering died in 1655, and the house passed into the hands of his son John. The younger John added a two-story wing on its eastern side in 1671. The dwelling then remained largely unchanged until 1751, when another addition, this one in the rear of the building, was erected by the second John's grandson Timothy Pickering. Two generations later Timothy's grandson John added the finials, gingerbread trim, and other delightful gothic elements that adorn the house today.

In 1951 the ancient house was deeded over to a nonprofit charitable trust known as the Pickering Foundation to be used as an educational and historical resource. The house, with its valuable collection of colonial furniture and other artifacts, was to be open to visitors on a limited basis, and the Pickering family was allowed to continue to live there.

Although the house underwent periodic physical changes over the centuries, one thing stayed the same. For more than three hundred and fifty years, until the string was broken in the late 1990s, the house was inhabited by eleven generations of Pickerings, all of them direct descendants of the original John Pickering. No other house in America can match this record of continuous family occupancy.

Puritan mores

In seventeenth-century Puritan Salem the rights of the society superceded those of the individual. Hardly any aspect of life, from dress to church attendance to the growing of tobacco, was free from legislation or institutional control.

Even the length of a man's hair was a matter for government scrutiny. In 1637 John Gatchall was fined ten shillings for a boundary violation. Inserted into the court record of the judgment was a clause: "And in case he shall cutt off his lonng hair of his head . . . in the meantime, shall have abated five shillings of his fine."

Quaker persecution

Usually lost in all the attention given the 1692 witch trials is the inhumane and brutal treatment suffered by the Quakers who came to Salem in the late 1650s. Quaker missionaries and their local followers posed a serious threat to the Congregationalist-dominated power structure. The Massachusetts General Court,

Usually a very modest woman, Deborah Wilson, a convert to Quakerism, decided to stroll through the town naked to make the point that the Congregational church was bare. She was arrested and tried by the local courts. Her punishment was designed to fit her crime.

or legislature, quickly passed laws in 1658 that made it illegal for the Friends to gather for worship. In the ensuing few years, until King Charles II intervened in 1661, the upstart Quakers often were flogged, sometimes until the flesh hung off their backs. Some had their ears cut off or had holes bored through their tongues. Others were put to death by local authorities.

One of the more unusual incidents that took place during the Quaker persecution involved Deborah Wilson. Usually a very modest woman, Deborah, a convert to Quakerism, decided to stroll through Salem naked to make the point that the Congregational church was bare. She was arrested and tried by the local courts. Her punishment was designed to fit her crime. She and her Quaker mother and sister were to be escorted through town topless and flogged up to thirty lashes.

Constable Daniel Rumball, who was to carry out the sentence, asked to be relieved of his duty, but his request was denied by the court. The constable and Wilson's husband Robert then worked out a plan to spare Deborah the thirty lashes. Robert accompanied his wife as she was led through town. Each time the constable snapped the whip in Deborah's direction, her husband clapped his hat with his hand to imitate the sound of the whip hitting flesh.

Buying the land

One morning in 1684 the people of Salem awoke to find themselves residents of a new colony. King Charles II had grown tired of the Massachusetts Bay Colony's independent and often disobedient behavior. The monarch had finally revoked the charter that gave the colony the right to exist.

Massachusetts was now united with the colonies of New Jersey, New York, Maine, Plymouth, Connecticut, New Haven, and Rhode Island as a single entity, the Dominion of New England. A royal governor, Sir Edmund Andros, was later appointed to rule the colony.

Andros had almost unlimited power. He could levy taxes, promote the Church of England, and cancel land grants. The colonists most feared the possibility that their property deeds would be declared null and void by the new administration.

The colonists desperately needed some legal basis for their claims of land ownership. On October 11, 1686, the selectmen of the town of Salem purchased from David Nonnupanohow, Sarah Wuttaquatimnusk, and other surviving heirs of Native American chiefs, the land that the settlers had occupied and distributed among themselves for nearly six decades.

The land in question encompasses what is today Salem, Danvers, and Peabody. The cost? A paltry twenty pounds.

Spectral and legal assaults

Despite its remarkable maritime history, architectural treasures, and claim to native son Nathaniel Hawthorne, Salem is best known in most parts of the world for its infamous witch trials in 1692.

Much of the early activity during the Salem witch trials actually took place in Salem Village, now Danvers, where the conflict began. The trials and executions, however, took place in Salem. So did some of the more bizarre episodes that were alleged to have occurred.

One of these involved John Louder and accused witch Bridget Bishop. Louder worked for John Gedney, Jr., whose property abutted Bishop's on the southeast corner of Washington and Church Streets.

The incidents referred to in Louder's testimony allegedly took place a few years prior to 1692, while Bridget was still living in Salem. Bishop's fowl, young Louder testified, frequently strayed into the Gedney orchard and became such a nuisance that he eventually confronted Bishop, and an argument ensued.

Louder claimed that shortly after their confrontation he awoke in the middle of the night to find either Bishop or her specter sitting on his stomach. Taking his throat in her hands, the witch began to choke him. Louder tried to push her off but found he had "no strength or power in my hands to resist, or help myself; and in this condition, she held me almost to day."

John told his employers what had happened. Susannah Gedney confronted Bridget Bishop with Louder's story, but Bishop denied it. Soon after, as Louder testified, he stayed home from meeting on the Sabbath because he wasn't feeling well. While lying in his bed with the doors and windows of his room closed, he "did see a black pig coming towards me; so I went towards it to kick it, and it vanished away."

But John would be left unmolested for just a short time. A "black thing" with the body of a monkey, a cock's clawed feet, and a face "somewhat more like a man's than a monkey's" appeared in the room. The creature proceeded to lecture Louder at length. Should he agree to be ruled by Satan, John was told, he would "want for nothing in this world."

"You Devil," Louder screamed in reply, "I will kill you." He swung at the creature but felt no flesh upon contact. The specter vanished out the window but immediately reentered the room through a closed door. Louder again lashed out at his assailant, this time with a stick, but again he did not make contact with a substance. The creature then vanished.

Shaken, John Louder opened the back door and went outside. He spied Bridget Bishop walking toward her house, and attempted to follow her. But he found he was unable to move in her direction.

John then returned to the house. As he was about to close

John Westgate testified that he was making his way home when "I heard a great noise; and there appeared a black hog running towards me with an open mouth as though he would have devoured me at that instant time."

the door, he spotted the monkey-like creature looking like it was about to attack again.

"The whole armor of God be between me and you," shrieked Louder. At this the beast "sprang back and flew over the apple tree, flinging the dirt with its feet against my stomach, upon which I was struck dumb; and so continued for about three days' time; and also shook many of the apples off from the tree which it flew over," Louder later testified.

For John Louder, it had been a very bad day. But his tormenter would soon have an even worse one. In June 1692 Bridget Bishop, having been convicted of the crime of witchcraft on the strength of the testimony of John Louder and others, was transported in a heavily guarded cart to Gallows Hill and hanged.

The fate of Alice Parker, the wife of a Salem fisherman, was sealed by testimony about another alleged incident.

Parker's husband, John, frequented Samuel Beadle's tavern on Prison Lane, now St. Peter Street. One night, fed up with her husband's absence from home, Alice went to Beadle's to fetch him.

At the tavern the unhappy housewife proceeded to berate her husband in front of his drinking companions. One of these men, John Westgate, scolded her for "unbeseeming" behavior. Westgate later testified that Alice then "bid me mind my own business, and told me I had better have said nothing."

Later Westgate would testify that one night sometime after the incident at the tavern he was making his way home along Essex Street when, just as he reached what is today the corner of Washington Square East, he "heard a great noise; and there appeared a black hog running towards me with an open mouth as though he would have devoured me at that instant time."

A terrified Westgate took to flight, but after a short distance he tumbled to the ground. As he fell his sheathed knife tore his hip. With blood flowing down his leg, he crawled along the fence to his home with the hog following behind menacingly. John managed to reach home without any further injury.

Shortly after that night John Westgate swore out a complaint against Alice Parker for witchcraft, alleging that the offending hog was Goody Parker or another evil creature doing her bidding. He based his assumption largely on the behavior of his "stout dog" who had a reputation for assaulting or otherwise worrying real hogs. But the very sight of the black hog that attacked his master made the cur run away, "leaping over the fence and crying much."

John Westgate's evidence helped send Alice Parker to her death on September 22, 1692.

In writing about the case nearly two centuries later, Charles Upham opined that the reason for the dog's frightened behavior that night was actually the bizarre antics of his master, John Westgate, not the appearance of a spectral hog.

English vs. Corwin

Phillip English, a Salem merchant and one of the richest men in the Massachusetts Bay Colony, was accused with his wife of witchcraft in 1692.

Thanks to Phillip's wealth and political power, the couple avoided Gallows Hill. They were imprisoned in Boston but were permitted to roam free during the day as long as they returned to the jail at night. The Englishes were later provided with a carriage in which to escape and a letter of introduction from the governor of Massachusetts to his counterpart in New York.

After the witch trials ended, the pair returned to Salem only to find that the bulk of their fortune had been seized by Sheriff George Corwin. English sued Corwin to recover his confiscated property and otherwise made life miserable for the former sheriff.

The aggrieved merchant got little satisfaction from the courts. So when George Corwin died in 1697, English threatened to seize the body and hold it until his claims were satisfied. The Corwin family buried George on his own property for safekeeping and eventually settled with Phillip English for a paltry £60.

The Witch Trial Memorial

❧

Three hundred years would pass before the city of Salem erected an official memorial to the innocent victims of the 1692 witch trials.

Such a memorial would have been installed more than 150 years earlier had the town fathers listened to author Nathaniel Hawthorne. In "Alice Doane's Appeal," one of his earliest surviving stories, Hawthorne called for a monument to be built on the summit of Gallows Hill "in dark, funereal stone" and "commemorative of the errors of an earlier race."

Hawthorne, incidentally, also suggested, in his story "A Rill from the Town Pump," that a monument be built to honor the pump that had provided fresh water to Salemites for more than two centuries. That wish was fulfilled when a fountain was erected in Town House Square in the early 1970s.

In 1944 the city of Salem's plans to widen North and Essex Streets threatened the Corwin house. Historic Salem, Inc., was established by the city to oversee the moving and restoration of both this structure and the adjacent Bowditch house.

Restoring the Witch House

❧

At the corner of North and Essex Streets, in the long shadow of Gallows Hill, stands the Witch House, the former home of witch trial judge Jonathan Corwin.

Corwin was a wealthy merchant and a political and military leader in seventeenth-century Salem. He acquired this multi-gabled house from the estate of Nathaniel Davenport in 1675 and hired carpenter Daniel Andrew to finish and remodel the dwelling. Andrew would be accused of witchcraft during the 1692 Salem witch trials but would escape to Europe.

Jonathan Corwin served on the Court of Oyer and Terminer that sent twenty innocent people to their deaths for the alleged crime of witchcraft in 1692. He and John Hathorne and Bartholomew Gedney conducted many of the pretrial hearings of the accused.

Yet Corwin displayed an obvious lack of enthusiasm for the witch hunt. He seemed content to take notes and just watch the chaos swirling about the court. His passivity prompted the afflicted girls to accuse Jonathan's mother-in-law, Margaret Thacher, of witchcraft. But she was never arrested.

After the witch trials finally ended in May 1693, Jonathan Corwin went on to serve in a number of important judicial and political posts in the colonial government. He died in 1718.

The Corwin House stayed in the family for more than a century after Jonathan's death and underwent a number of structural changes. His grandson George's widow, Sarah, replaced the pitched roof with a gambrel and added a rear lean-to in 1746. A later owner, druggist George Farrington, built an addition on the front, eastern side of the house.

In 1944 the city of Salem's plans to widen North and Essex Streets threatened the Corwin house. Historic Salem, Inc., was established by the city to oversee the moving and restoration of both this structure and the adjacent Bowditch house.

According to Olive Bogart, whose father William was part of the restoration team, the Corwin house, chimney and all, was moved in a cradle some forty feet. Workmen then dug up the hearths at the old location.

"Under the hearth of one of the fireplaces they found bones," wrote Olive Bogart in an article in *Yankee* magazine. "These were sent somewhere to determine their origin, whether to the Medical Examiner, Harvard College, or the Animal Rescue League, is uncertain."

The results of the tests, wherever they may have been conducted, were never made public. The origin of the bones remains a mystery today, more than a half-century later.

Eighteenth Century

One local loyalist who paid a dear price for his allegiance to the King was Nathaniel Ropes. As animosity toward Tories reached a fever pitch in 1774, Ropes, a superior court judge under the Royal government, resigned his position. But his resignation didn't satisfy Salem patriots; nothing less than a renunciation of the Royal government would suffice. In March an angry mob stormed Ropes's mansion on Essex Street.

The Codfish Aristocracy

❧

Concurrent with the Salem witch trials were the French and Indian Wars which had erupted in 1689 and would continue intermittently for a quarter of a century. The conflict wreaked havoc on the Salem fishing industry and maritime trade. At one point the town had lost fifty-four of its approximately sixty vessels.

The signing of the Treaty of Utrecht in 1713 brought a temporary end to the French and Indian Wars. The treaty gave colonial fishermen the right to fish the waters of the bountiful Grand Banks off the coast of Nova Scotia. In the twenty-five years following the cessation of hostilities, a number of local merchants accumulated great wealth by exporting salted codfish to the West Indies and Europe. This elite group came to be known as the "codfish aristocracy."

Benjamin Pickman, Jr., was one of the town's preeminent merchants. When Pickman built his new mansion on a lot that is now occupied by the Peabody Essex Museum's Japanese garden, he had a gilt wooden codfish placed on the riser of each stair in the house. The merchant, it was said, wished to remain mindful of the source of the wealth that made his magnificent mansion possible.

Church conflict and separation

✧

The political and social upheaval that would characterize Salem in the mid-eighteenth century was mirrored in its churches.

In the years between 1718 and 1772 three new Congregational churches were founded in Salem by parishioners who had abandoned the First Church. Sometimes the separation went smoothly; sometimes it didn't.

The events leading to the creation of what is today called the Tabernacle Church were most unchristian. In the late 1720s First Church minister John Fisk became involved in a lengthy dispute with some of his parishioners. At issue was Fisk's unilateral decision to discontinue the practice of holding Lecture Day, a second mandatory day at church, on a regular basis.

Over time the dispute escalated. When Fisk's supporters and foes failed to resolve their conflict internally, the matter was turned over to a council of churches. That body's binding decision, rendered in October 1734, was in favor of Mr. Fisk's opponents.

The minister and his supporters refused to abide by the decision and continued to hold services in the meeting house in Town House Square. The dissident faction, which represented only one-quarter of the congregation but had the power of the council behind it, eventually voted to remove Fisk as minister of the First Church. They physically barred him and his followers from entering the meeting house.

Fisk's supporters then organized a new church, which they called the First Church, and erected a house of worship near what is now 256 Essex Street, just over fifty yards from their original home.

It would be a quarter of a century before the two congregations reconciled. At a meeting in 1762, Fisk's congregation relinquished the rights to the First Church name and turned over the church records it had taken at the time of separation. The two sides also divided silver and other property that had belonged to the original First Church.

Curiously, the two other congregations that separated from the First Church in the decades before the American Revolution later returned. The East Church, later known as the Second Church, was organized in 1713 and rejoined the First Church in 1956. The North Church separated from the First Church in 1772 and was reunited in 1923.

Fires and fire clubs

A young lad was just doing his assigned chore, sweeping the classrooms of the Salem Grammar School, when he spotted a rat racing across the floor and down into a hole.

The youngster retrieved a glowing coal from the stove and threw it down the hole, hoping to burn the rodent to death. The result was predictable. Much of the school and the adjoining library went up in flames.

Fires, no matter what the cause, were a major concern in towns like Salem in the seventeenth and eighteenth centuries when wood was the construction material of choice.

In 1744 Edward Holyoke, Benjamin Pickman, Jr., William Browne, and other prominent Salemites organized "The Old Fire Club." Each member was required to keep a leather or cedar fire bucket handy to be used in the event that a fire broke out on the premises of any one of its members. Club members also met for social purposes three times a year.

The Union Fire Club was the next to organize, in 1748. The following year it received permission from the town to buy and operate Salem's first fire engine. The simple apparatus consisted of a large box, mounted on wooden wheels, which was filled with buckets of water. The water shot out of a pipe that was located at the top of the box. Propulsion was provided by a hand-operated pump.

The worst fire in the annals of colonial Salem occurred on the night of October 6, 1774. The Tabernacle Church and dozens of other buildings in the vicinity of Town House Square went up in flames. The roof of the Town House caught fire, but the flames were quickly extinguished with the help of Marbleheaders who had responded to a request for help.

It was a good thing they did. The very next day the patriotic members of the Massachusetts General Court met in the Town House—as planned—and reorganized as a revolutionary Provincial Congress.

Shortly after the inferno, the town sponsored a thank-you breakfast for the Marbleheaders who had provided assistance. It must have been quite an event. Caterer John Webb was reimbursed for 132 breakfasts, three gallons of West Indian rum, and three gallons of gin.

Extreme weather

The pages of Reverend Joseph Felt's *Annals of Salem,* a two-volume collection of historical facts about the town that was published in 1827 and 1828, are filled with fascinating tidbits about weather extremes and other oddities in Salem's history.

In July 1773 lightning struck a tree on Gallows Hill and rendered it the shape of a broom. In 1798 another bolt hit the ship *Martha* in Salem Harbor, killing two sailors and wounding two others.

Salem experienced a violent hailstorm on August 1, 1815. Some hailstones were five inches in circumference. The storm lasted but a few minutes but broke thirty thousand panes of glass in Salem alone. Every house in the town lost at least one pane. A similar storm in 1819 destroyed 168 panes of glass in a single home on Essex Street. Felt notes: "Human power quailed before its violence."

Snowstorms in 1829 and 1978 dumped at least two feet of the white stuff on Salem in a single day. And in what had been a normal July in 1804, snow fell one day in Salem and surrounding towns.

Salem has experienced hurricanes, blizzards, earthquakes, eclipses, and many other natural phenomena. But to local townspeople nothing was as frightening as the "great darkness" that fell over the town on May 19, 1780.

According to an entry in the diary of William Pyncheon, the darkness began descending over the town at ten in the morning on that normal, bright day. Over the next two hours the sky grew increasingly dark, and by noon people were eating and reading by candlelight. Confused cocks crowed, and a general melancholy fell over the townspeople—except the sailors, who went "halloing" through the streets and taunting the young ladies they encountered to divest themselves of some of their clothing.

Members of Dr. Nathaniel Whitaker's church gathered for solace at their meeting house on School Street, now Washington Street. Instead they were rebuked by their pastor, who claimed the darkness was a punishment sent from the Lord for past transgressions.

The darkness, incidentally, was caused by the smoke from wildfires in northern New England.

After he was identified as an informer, Thomas Rowe was taken by a local mob to the Salem common, where he was tarred and feathered. He was then placed in a cart, and, wearing a placard that read INFORMER, he was transported to the western end of Essex Street. Thomas was then forced to walk the gauntlet while a live and angry goose was hurled at him.

Patriot fervor

In the decade leading up to the Revolutionary War, Salem became a major hotbed of patriotism. The atmosphere toward local supporters of the Crown became increasingly hostile.

Thomas Rowe was one of the first loyalists to feel the wrath of the local radicals. Rowe had tattled on a vessel that was engaged in smuggling taxable goods. After he was identified as the informer, the unlucky Rowe was taken by a local mob to the Salem common, where he was tarred and feathered. He was then placed in a cart, and, wearing a placard that read INFORMER, he was transported to the western end of Essex Street. Thomas was then forced to walk the gauntlet while a live and angry goose was hurled at him.

Rowe shrewdly fled to Boston. The Royal government later compensated him for the loss of his job at the Salem Custom House.

Another local loyalist paid an even dearer price for his allegiance to the King. As animosity toward Tories reached a fever pitch in 1774, Nathaniel Ropes, a superior court judge under the Royal government, resigned his position. But his resignation did not satisfy Salem patriots; nothing less than a renunciation of the Royal government would suffice.

In March an angry mob stormed Ropes's mansion on Essex Street. Patriots hurled stones and bottles at the building as the family cowered inside. Some members of the mob pounded on the front door, demanding to see Judge Ropes. The judge, unfortunately, was too ill with smallpox to respond. In fact, he would die the next morning.

After that attack many Tories fled to Halifax, Nova Scotia, or to England. Others departed on the suggestion of the local patriots. Windows in the homes of Royalists William Browne and William Pyncheon were broken. Salem's Anglican church,

St. Peter's, was also vandalized, and by 1777 it was closed. Services would not resume until 1782.

Some Salem Tories suffered further damage when the provincial government passed the Conspiracy, Banishment, and Confiscation Acts in 1778 and 1779. These measures gave communities the right to banish any and all residents who were loyal to the Crown and to confiscate any property they might own. The most affected of the Salem Tories was William Brown. Under these acts, all his property was confiscated, and Browne himself was forbidden to return to Salem under penalty of death. But Browne landed on his feet. He received an appointment as Royal Governor of the British island of Bermuda.

The Revolution begins

❧

Should it care to press the issue, Salem could make a strong case for being the birthplace of the American Revolution.

After the Boston Tea Party, Governor Gage moved the Massachusetts seat of government to Salem. At its first session here, in June 1774, the Massachusetts General Court voted to send representatives to a Continental Congress to be held in Philadelphia. Gage then grew wary and decided to cancel the next session of the court, which was scheduled for early October.

Ninety representatives disregarded Gage's orders and gathered in the Town House at the corner of Essex and Court (now Washington) Streets. On the first day of the session no real business was transacted. But on the second day those present voted to reorganize as a Provincial Congress independent of royal authority. John Hancock was subsequently elected president, and the meeting was adjourned.

Four months after this act of bloodless revolution, Salem would be the site of the first armed resistance to British troops.

On February 26, 1775, nearly two months before the Battles of Lexington and Concord, local patriots faced off against more than two hundred British troops at Salem under the command of Lieutenant Colonel Alexander Leslie.

The Royals had been sent on a secret mission to capture cannon and ammunition the locals had hidden in North Salem. Leslie's troops landed in neighboring Marblehead on Sunday, February 26, when the population would be at church. Their movements were observed by heathens who spread the alarm.

Colonel John Pedrick of Marblehead was chosen to take the news to Salem because his daughter had been dating Leslie. Pedrick caught up with the advancing British column and exchanged pleasantries with the British colonel. Leslie then ordered his columns to let the Marbleheader pass.

This error in judgment on Leslie's part doomed the expedition. When the British arrived in Salem, the community was on full alert and a messenger was already on his way to warn surrounding towns. At the North River the British troops encountered an open drawbridge which the locals refused to lower when ordered to do so by Colonel Leslie.

For the next two hours on that bitter February afternoon the two sides exchanged threats, insults, and curses while shivering in the biting wind. As the afternoon wore on, militia outfits from local communities began to arrive. It soon became clear to Leslie that retreat was his best alternative. A face-saving agreement was reached by which the bridge was lowered and the British marched thirty rods into North Salem—to fulfill at least part of their orders—before turning around and returning to their waiting vessel in Marblehead.

Militia companies from Amesbury and Salisbury, on the border of Massachusetts and New Hampshire, started for Salem but got only as far as Newbury. There they heard that the issue at the North River had been settled. Before heading home the companies stopped in nearby Newburyport where they had been invited for a libation.

In his humorous account of what transpired in Newburyport, one William Gallison reported, "But bloodyminded men as they were, they resolved not to go home without doing some execution, and therefore they violently attacked and demolished several barrels, whose Precious blood they drew and entirely exhausted." When the barrels were empty, Gallison noted in his letter to his father, the militiamen "were scarce able to crawl home. . . . So much for this military Expedition."

Privateering and the Kirwan Library

Once the Revolutionary War began, Salem privateers took to sea in large numbers. During the course of the conflict, armed Salem ships captured or sank 445 British vessels.

A Beverly privateer made a special contribution to Salem during the Revolution. In 1781 the *Pilgrim,* owned by the Cabot brothers and commanded by Hugh Hill, was cruising in the English Channel when it came upon the heavily armed schooner *Mars.* After a brief skirmish, the *Mars* struck her colors.

The *Pilgrim* returned to Beverly in early February with its prize in tow. An inventory of the *Mars's* cargo turned up one of the world's greatest scientific libraries, a 116-volume collection of science and medical books owned by Dr. Richard Kirwan of Dublin, Ireland. The books had been en route to Kirwan's new residence in London.

An auction of the *Mars's* cargo was scheduled for mid-April. The Reverend Samuel Willard of Beverly was horrified to think that this priceless scientific library might be sold piecemeal at the auction. He enlisted other ministers, doctors, and men of letters from local communities in an attempt to save it.

Dr. John Prince of Salem represented the group at the auction. He managed to purchase almost the entire collection for just over £858. Another bidder acquired a few of the Kirwan books, but he was easily persuaded to resell them to Dr. Prince's group. The other bidder had only planned to use them for wrapping paper.

The Kirwan scientific collection provided the foundation for the new Philosophical Library, which would be housed permanently in Salem. In 1810 the library merged with the Social Library (founded in 1761) to create the Salem Athenaeum.

The new owners of the Kirwan library later contacted Dr. Kirwan, offering to pay for his priceless treasures. Kirwan generously declined the money, saying he was just happy the books were being used.

King Derby

Almost immediately after the American Revolution ended, England closed her ports to American vessels. Colonists had to find new trade routes. Elias Hasket Derby of Salem, flush with capital from years of successful privateering, led the way in developing those routes.

The Derbys were ardent patriots during the Revolution. Elias, who managed the family fleet, sent out twenty-five of the privateers that sailed from Salem during the course of the war and invested in or supplied as many as fifty others. Those vessels captured 144 British merchant ships.

Beginning in the mid-1780s the entrepreneur began sending ships to trade with India, China, the Philippines, Russia, and other nations around the globe. Derby also set up an overseas base of operations in India and sent his son to manage it.

Elias Derby was a true innovator. He was one of the first merchants to employ business agents, or supercargoes, on his ships, and he even helped design those ships. He played a key role in convincing the federal government to establish bonded warehouses, where merchants could store imported goods and not pay the assessed duty until the selling market was favorable enough to offer the goods for sale.

During his tenure as head of the Derby fleet, Elias employed an estimated 1300 seamen. Up through the Derby ranks came the likes of future U.S. Senator Nathaniel Silsbee; the great navigator Nathaniel Bowditch; and Joseph Peabody, who would ultimately eclipse Elias Derby, at least statistically, as the greatest Salem merchant of them all.

Derby set an admirable standard for the treatment of seamen. In an industry where one merchant, hearing one of his vessels had sunk with all hands aboard, commented, "Well at least it was insured," Derby stood out as a man who provisioned his ship with fresh vegetables and took care of the families of employees who died or were disabled. Derby also refused to traffic in slaves.

His respect for others and his standing in the town earned the merchant the nickname "King." Few cared that his eyes were two different colors, one blue and one brown.

In 1762 Elias Derby married Elizabeth Crowninshield, whose father and brothers would be among the most successful merchants in Salem in the early nineteenth century. The couple lived in a number of homes on the waterfront in downtown Salem. Their final residence was the magnificent mansion designed for them by both Charles Bulfinch and Samuel McIntire and built in what we know call Derby Square. Elias Derby died in that mansion shortly after taking up residence in 1799.

A list of the forty richest Americans of all time published in *American Heritage* magazine in 1998 ranked Derby number thirty-nine. Derby made plenty of money in the maritime trade in his lifetime, some say $800,000, some say $1 million.

Exactly how much "King" Derby made hardly matters. What does matter are his contributions to Salem's rise to preeminence as one of the busiest and wealthiest shipping ports in America. Today the city's main waterfront thoroughfare and historic district bear the Derby name, a tribute to one of Salem's greatest citizens.

A Derby postscript

Walter Merrill, former director of the Essex Institute, told this story during a talk at Governor Dummer Academy in 1957.

Three Salem women had just concluded a committee meeting and were discussing where to go for a libation. One of them, a native Southerner, remembered that the Kentucky Derby was about to get under way on television. "It's Derby Day!" said she. "Let's go to the Hawthorne Hotel and have a cocktail."

"Oh!" exclaimed one of her companions. "I hadn't realized it was Elias Haskett Derby's birthday!"

Nathaniel Silsbee, master

One of Elias Derby's prized protégés was Nathaniel Silsbee, who started out as a cabin boy on a Derby ship and ended up serving as U.S. Senator from Massachusetts.

Silsbee was born in 1773, and like many Salem boys he left school and shipped out at age fourteen. By the time he was nineteen, Elias Derby trusted him enough to make him captain of the 161-ton ship *Benjamin* bound for the Cape of Good Hope and India.

On its first night out of port the *Benjamin* encountered a bitterly cold storm. Most of the crew retreated below deck for the night, but the cook chose to sleep in his cooking house topside. As a result he suffered a bad case of frostbite that soon developed into gangrene.

It soon became obvious that the toes on both of the cook's feet needed to be amputated. No one else was willing to take on the brutal task, so it fell to nineteen-year-old Captain Silsbee. With only scissors and a razor for instruments, Nathaniel removed the toes from the very weak patient over the course of two agonizing days.

A few days later a surgeon from an English frigate came aboard to examine the patient and pronounced the operation a success. Within two weeks the cook was back at work.

On a later voyage Captain Silsbee was returning home aboard a vessel he had purchased in Ile de France when he became suspicious of a schooner that appeared to be following him. Nathaniel issued orders to the crew to prepare the vessel for possible combat.

A few members of the crew protested. They had been hired to sail, not to fight, they claimed, and they refused to help. Silsbee immediately ordered all the hatches that led below deck to be fastened to prevent the recalcitrant crew members from hiding. The young skipper then ordered the mutineers up into the shrouds, where they would be the most vulnerable if the ship were attacked, to make unnecessary repairs to the masts and sails.

Silsbee's strategy worked. As the enemy vessel drew closer, the mutineers decided they would be much safer on deck if and when the fighting began. They scrambled down the mast and joined their fellow crew members in preparing for the defense of their vessel.

Eventually Nathaniel had saved enough money to become part owner of a vessel, the *Portland*. On his new ship's next voyage he served as captain. In the course of the trip the *Portland* was captured by a French privateer and escorted to Málaga. The harbor was filled with vessels of various nations awaiting the outcome of condemnation hearings conducted by French authorities.

Silsbee was taken ashore with his ship's papers. There he was subjected to a brutal interrogation by an arrogant French consul who demanded that Nathaniel answer his questions in five words or less. Silsbee agreed to provide the information requested. But, he bluntly told the consul, he would do so in as many words as he needed.

At the conclusion of the hearing, the official informed Captain Silsbee that he could return to his vessel and await a decision about his ship's fate. The deliberations, the consul said, would take at least a month and maybe as many as three.

Silsbee was furious. He found the time frame intolerable and refused to leave the office until a decision was made. When consular staff departed at midnight, Silsbee was still ensconced in the office. He was still there when they returned at nine in the morning.

Nathaniel sat silent and resolute throughout the day. He left the consul's office briefly, long enough to file a formal protest, and then resumed his sit-in in the consul's office. Finally, at nine o'clock that evening, after Silsbee had endured forty hours without food or sleep, the consul cracked. The plucky captain's papers were returned to him along with permission to sail.

Silsbee's stubbornness had paid off handsomely. Every other vessel in the harbor was ultimately condemned and sold at auction.

A few years and a few voyages later, Nathaniel Silsbee retired from the sea to his mansion on Washington Square in Salem. He oversaw the business affairs of his growing fleet until he was drafted by local residents to run for public office. Silsbee would eventually be elected to both houses of the Massachusetts and U.S. legislatures.

Mutiny at sea

☙

The sea captain's world was far less glamorous and much more dangerous than novels and movies lead us to believe. And in real life the story's ending was not always good.

Masters of Salem ships found plenty of danger in their travels; pirates, cannibals, disease, shipwreck, enemy naval vessels, and even unscrupulous merchants all posed threats to their crew's safety and their mission. But oftentimes a captain of a vessel found the most serious threat right onboard his own ship—his crew members.

Nathaniel Garland, master of the Salem schooner *Tattler*, was below deck in his cabin one evening in 1823 when he heard a scream for help. Garland raced up the companionway to the deck, where he found his first mate bleeding to death from stab wounds. The captain himself was then set upon by a knife-wielding crew member. While two other sailors stood by, Garland fought for his life.

The captain finally succeeded in wresting the weapon from his assailant and tossed it overboard. He raced to his cabin for a gun, and when he returned to the deck another life-and-death struggle ensued with his original assailant. The conflict ended when Garland sent the sailor over the railing, as he had the knife a few minutes earlier.

Captains had to be quick and decisive in dealing with rebellious or violent seamen. When crew members aboard the Salem vessel *Beaver* refused to surrender a bottle of rum, the first mate took it by force and prepared to flog the ringleader of the unruly group.

As the floggee was being tied to the mast in preparation for receiving his punishment, his friends advanced on the captain, Richard Cleveland, with daggers in hand. In a scene right out of the movies, Cleveland coolly laid a piece of rope on the deck between the two parties. With a pistol in each hand, Cleveland faced the hostile seamen and dared any and all to step across it. The flogging then proceeded without interruption. Cleveland had no further trouble with the crew.

Perhaps the most incredible story relating to a mutinous crew appears in *Memories of Old Salem* by Mary Northend. According to the author in her chapter about ships' figureheads, the sailors aboard an unnamed vessel decided to become pirates. When the captain and first mate realized that the crew planned to seize the ship, the two men retreated to the cabin and held the rogues at bay with loaded muskets.

The trapped men then designed a brilliant but risky plan of escape. The first mate created a diversion at the starboard window, attracting the attention of the mutineers. As soon as the coast was clear, the captain climbed out the port window of the cabin and raced to the bow of the vessel. In his hand he carried a bucket of black paint and a brush.

When the would-be pirates spotted the captain, they followed him to the front of the ship. As they approached him, the captain raised the paintbrush and threatened to repaint the beautiful female figurehead that graced the vessel's bowsprit.

The mutineers, like most superstitious sailors, believed that something terrible would happen to a ship if its figurehead was damaged or altered in any way. They dropped to their knees in front of the captain and "promised submission if only he would relinquish his fatal purpose." The mutiny was ended.

One of the most famous insurrections that occurred on a Salem vessel involved not the crew but a "cargo" of slaves who were being transported to America by Captain William Fairfield. In a letter dated April 23, 1789, Fairfield's son, who was also a member of the crew, sadly informed his mother that a month earlier five of the slaves on board had revolted and "killed my Honored Sire." The rebels had somehow gained possession of firearms and other weapons but were subdued after a brief skirmish. They were later sold into slavery.

Maritime nightmares

ભ્ર

A stroll down magnificent Chestnut Street or around Washington Square provides adequate evidence that many a fortune was made in Salem's lucrative maritime trade. Mansions erected by merchants such as Nathaniel Silsbee, John Gardner, and Joseph Hodges were financed by the tremendous profits made from trading voyages to Europe and to both the East and West Indies in the decades following the American Revolution.

But those riches were often obtained at great risk to the men who actually went to sea. Some crew members aboard local vessels doing business in the cannibal-ridden Fiji Islands ended up in what Samuel Eliot Morison once called "Salem Stew." Others were enslaved in northern Africa or slaughtered by creese-wielding Malays while buying pepper in Sumatra.

For one Salem seaman named Samuel Becket, the real threat to his life came in the shape of the captain of the vessel on which Becket was serving in March 1804.

The brig *William and Charles* was on a voyage to the West Indies, a popular trade destination for Salem vessels. One afternoon Becket was awakened from a sound sleep to find Captain Gould stealing his pistols from his seaman's chest. The sailor and Gould had feuded earlier in the day, and as he grabbed the pistols out of the captain's hands, Becket asked if the captain planned to kill him.

A few hours later, feeling safe because the vessel was approaching its anchorage, Becket lay back down to sleep. All of a sudden the sailor woke with a start. Captain Gould was in the process of slashing his throat with a razor. Becket managed to escape into the steerage, but the captain followed and, as Becket lay on the ground bleeding, the captain began slicing the back of his neck. Before the razor-wielding madman could cause any further damage, crew members tackled him.

Mercifully, Becket received prompt medical attention and lived to tell his tale. Gould was deemed insane and left in confinement in Surinam in South America.

One fear local sailors lived with was of being captured by, and being made to serve on, the naval vessels of a hostile nation. This practice, known as impressment, was especially common in times of conflict.

James Barnes of Salem was impressed onto a British vessel in 1796 and forced to fight in engagements against the French Navy. When an American vessel came into view one day, Barnes and a shipmate jumped overboard and swam to it. But when they arrived at the American ship, they were not allowed to board. The American captain feared that if he abetted their escape, the British would retaliate by bombarding his vessel.

The two men had no choice but to return to the English ship. Barnes's companion never made it—he was eaten by a shark en route. The Salem man did reboard the ship, and after suffering many other indignities he finally made his way back to Salem.

Benjamin Ober was onboard a Salem vessel that sank off Cape Cod in a February storm in 1802. He washed ashore, where he spent thirty-six hours buried up to his neck in sand. He was finally rescued but died soon after.

Occasionally what appeared to be a maritime tragedy had a happy ending.

Peter Jackson was serving as a cook on the *Ceres* out of Salem. Near Calcutta, he was washed overboard and presumed drowned or eaten by crocodiles. But Jackson survived and found his way home on another vessel. He reappeared on the streets of Salem, frightening half to death a former shipmate who thought he was seeing a ghost.

The two American sailors had no choice but to return to the English ship.
Barnes's companion never made it—he was eaten by a shark en route.

Bowditch brings home the *Putnam*

Under normal circumstances the crew of the *Putnam* would have had no chance of getting home to their families for Christmas dinner.

The *Putnam*, Nathaniel Bowditch master, had just survived a five-month voyage that should have taken three. On its return trip from the East Indies, the Salem vessel had encountered and survived one hair-raising storm after another. Just a few miles from Derby Wharf and home, she was stalled in a fog bank that was so thick the sailors could barely see the top of the mainmast or the tip of the bowsprit.

Adding to their predicament were the many small islands and hidden ledges dotting Salem Sound, which rendered navigation treacherous under normal conditions. Indeed, just a few years earlier three vessels had sunk in the waters off Baker's Island in a period of a few months.

Any other captain would have dropped anchor until the fog lifted. But Nathaniel Bowditch was not any captain. He was a self-made scientist who was in the process of rewriting the book on navigation.

As a young man Nat had taught himself mathematics, astronomy, and navigation in his free time while working as an apprentice clerk in Ropes and Hodges's ship chandlery. Before he was twenty Bowditch had solved the centuries-old problem of how to determine longitude without a clock or chronometer or using dead reckoning.

When his apprenticeship ended in 1796, Nathaniel shipped out on the *Henry* as a ship's clerk. At sea the young scientist began testing his system of celestial navigation, which involved measuring the distance between the moon and a passing star with a sextant and then consulting pre-calculated tables to determine one's longitude.

The results confirmed what Nathaniel already knew. Any system based on mathematics was to be trusted unless human error was introduced. Bowditch had recently found and corrected more than eight thousand errors in the widely used tables compiled by John Hamilton Moore. His corrections had earned the twenty-seven-year-old membership in the prestigious American Academy of Arts and Sciences.

Yet convincing uneducated mariners and shipowners to adopt his methods had proven difficult, even after Bowditch had used his navigation system successfully on three voyages aboard Elias Derby's *Astrea*. But reluctance had gradually given way to acceptance, at least for those shipmates who attended Nathaniel's onboard navigation workshops.

Those working sessions helped Bowditch, too. The mathematical genius who would later be called "the first of New England's great scientists" by Dirk Struik in *Yankee Science in the Making*, learned how to communicate his knowledge to men who had little formal education. It wasn't surprising that his soon-to-be-published book *The New American Practical Navigator* would become essential reading for sailors in the future. The day would come when a boy would head to sea with "A Bible, a Bowditch, a trunk, and a mother's blessing."

But those days lay behind and ahead of Bowditch. On Christmas Day in 1803 he was putting his navigational abilities to the ultimate test. And his crew members were terrified. Although they were as anxious to get home for Christmas dinner as their captain, they feared the disorienting fog and hidden shoals and ledges.

Nathaniel Bowditch had already decided to press forward. A day earlier he had taken two shots at the sun with his sextant and had pinpointed his exact location in Massachusetts Bay. Armed with that information, accurate charts, and a compass, he believed he could get the *Putnam* home safely.

Using the time-honored log-and-line method of determining the vessel's speed, and lead lines to verify the water's depth, Bowditch zigged and zagged his way through Salem Sound. The

Putnam passed Bowditch's Ledge, supposedly named for an ancestor who had sunk a vessel on it, and the lighthouse on the western end of Baker's Island. The light, faintly visible in the darkness and the enveloping fog, would be one of the few visual landmarks the crew would see on its tense journey into Salem Harbor.

Nathaniel kept one eye on the compass and the other on the chart of Salem Harbor. He stayed in constant communication with the men measuring cruising speed and depth, and he issued change-of-direction commands to the crew.

The *Putnam* slid by Winter Island and the Crowninshield family's India Wharf somewhere off to the ship's starboard side, and suddenly the men were home.

This seemingly miraculous feat of navigation made Nathaniel Bowditch a legend in maritime circles. Many sailors and their families were just happy to be together on Christmas night.

George Washington visits Salem

ༀ

Salem has played host to many sitting U.S. presidents. John Quincy Adams came for the dedication of the East India Marine Hall in 1825, James Monroe for the opening of the new Town House and Market in 1817. William Howard Taft was involved in a car accident on Essex Street in 1911. And in the summer of 1925, President and Mrs. Calvin Coolidge were frequently seen on the streets of Salem.

Other chief executives have also come to Salem, but no presidential visit stirred more excitement and affection than that of George Washington.

The nation's beloved first chief executive was touring the new republic, and Salem's status as a leading port guaranteed it a spot on the president's itinerary. On the morning of October 29, 1789, President Washington left Boston for Salem. After brief

On his way to Beverly, President George Washington stopped briefly on the new Essex Bridge to examine the structure and its draw mechanism. The president's entourage, the Gazette noted, "passed [the bridge] free of toll."

stops in Lynn and Marblehead, the president arrived at the Salem-Marblehead line, where he was met by the Committee of Arrangements that had organized the events related to his visit.

Washington's arrival was acknowledged by a salute from the cannon at Winter Island. The president then left his carriage and mounted a white horse. The procession proceeded to town accompanied by the continuous pealing of church bells.

Washington greeted the assembled military regiments on Federal Street and continued on to Buffum's Corner. There he joined the officials and inhabitants gathered for the grand parade. The assembled marchers then escorted their beloved president to the court house at the intersection of present-day Church and Washington Streets.

Mr. Northey, the chairman of the selectmen, greeted the president at the court house. The Quaker grasped the president's gloved hand and said, "Friend Washington, we are glad to see thee, and in behalf of the inhabitants I bid thee a hearty welcome to Salem."

Washington was then seated in the second-floor balcony of the court house. He received the welcome and affection of the townspeople below and returned the same. Following the brief ceremony, the Salem Cadets, a volunteer military company, escorted the president to his lodgings at the home of Joshua Ward at the foot of Washington Street. There President Washington rested and received visitors until the evening concert at the Assembly House.

As the president left the Ward House for the concert that night, thirteen rockets were fired in the air, and thirteen more were set off when he arrived at the hall on Federal Street. At the Assembly House, Washington mingled with Salem's finest citizens and joined the daughter of his close friend Stephen Abbott of Salem in a dance. Being less than light on his feet, the president passed his winsome partner on to his aide Henry Knox.

Washington departed the following morning at nine for points east. On his way to Beverly, he stopped briefly on the new

Essex Bridge to examine the structure and its draw mechanism. The president's entourage, the *Gazette* noted, "passed [the bridge] free of toll."

Sort of. It seems that the management company that maintained the span and oversaw the collection of the tolls wasn't consulted before the fee was waived for Washington's entourage. The company summarily billed the bridge owners for the portion of the fee that they would have received had the president's party paid.

An execution and the *Essex*

៚

In 1772, when the population of Salem was approximately 6,500, a crowd of 12,000 showed up to see Bryan Sheehan hanged for rape on Salem Neck. Sheehan exhorted the gathered multitude to avoid the type of bad companions who had led him to ruination.

A similar-sized crowd assembled on the neck in 1799 for a far more joyful occasion—the launching of the *Essex*. The 850-ton frigate had been built on Winter Island under the supervision of master shipbuilder Enos Briggs and financed by donations from the people of Salem. All the materials used in her construction came from Essex County.

The *Essex* would prove to be one of America's greatest warships. The frigate was given to the U.S. government immediately after launching and helped bring an end to the harassment of American merchant vessels by the French Navy.

During the War of 1812 the *Essex,* under Captain David Porter, destroyed or captured almost the entire British whaling fleet then operating in the waters near South America.

The *Essex's* illustrious career ended in 1814 when she was cornered and nearly sunk in Valparaíso Harbor—in the neutral nation of Chile—by two British warships.

Nineteenth Century

As he was preparing to sail on the Charles Dogget *on January, 13, 1831, a group of townswomen presented Captain William Driver with an American flag. In response, the captain raised his hat in salute, saying, "My ship, my country, and my flag, Old Glory."*

A success story

❦

He shipped out for the first time at the age of sixteen as a cabin boy on the *Monkey*. Later in the voyage he transferred to a privateer that was captured by the British. He was briefly held captive on a prison ship in Bermuda and Barbados until his ability to speak fluent French (his family was originally from the Isle of Jersey) convinced his jailers that he was not an American, and he was subsequently released. He started for home aboard an American schooner, which also was taken by a British naval vessel. By the time the captured crew reached England and a waiting prison, the War of 1812 had ended. Again the sailor headed home to Salem on an American vessel.

The ship docked in Boston. The young man, penniless and shoeless, walked barefoot back to Salem. He barely caught his breath before shipping out again.

The worst was behind him, however. The Salem boy grew into a man and climbed the ship's ladder to captain. Ultimately he would become one of Salem's preeminent shipowners and most valuable citizens.

This wealthy merchant, who once said he wanted to live only as long as he could be of service to his fellow man, organized and substantially funded the Salem Hospital and a home for aged men. He gave freely to almost anyone who asked, and after his death in 1880 his family donated his Essex Street mansion to the city of Salem to use as a public library.

His name was John Bertram.

William Driver, the *Bounty,* and "Old Glory"

∾

The voyage was to be Captain William Driver's last, the culmination of a very successful career. He had worked his way up from cabin boy to captain and made a fortune trading in bêche-de-mer, a delicacy found in the Fiji Islands and sold at a great profit in China and Japan.

As he was preparing to sail on the *Charles Dogget* on January, 13, 1831, a group of townswomen presented Driver with an American flag. In response, the captain raised his hat in salute, saying, "My ship, my country, and my flag, Old Glory."

From that moment on, both Driver and the American flag would be known as Old Glory.

William Driver's last voyage was both memorable and dangerous. A violent snowstorm almost sank the *Charles Dogget* the day after it left port. In the East Indies the vessel was boarded and almost captured by pirates.

Driver and his crew finally arrived in Matavai Bay, Tahiti, on July 17, 1831. There they were greeted by a party who claimed to be the descendants of the HMS *Bounty* mutineers. They told Driver they had abandoned their beloved Pitcairn Island six months earlier to escape a serious water shortage. A British vessel had transported the group to Tahiti and given them a six-month supply of provisions. But they had found little relief in their adopted home. Devout Christians, they were horrified by the immorality of the natives. They also feared for their lives because some of the Tahitian tribesmen had grown openly hostile toward them.

The Pitcairn Islanders were desperate to return to their former home, water or no water. Captain Driver believed that the

Charles Dogget had been spared in the earlier storm for a reason; perhaps it was so he could help these people. He agreed to shuttle the sixty-five "forelorn, helpless" humans 1,400 miles back to Pitcairn Island.

The journey was fraught with peril. The *Dogget* was too small to carry so many people, and it sat dangerously low in the water. Driver also had to cope with treacherous, unfamiliar waters and hidden coral reefs. Mercifully the weather cooperated and all hands survived the frightening twenty-one-day trip.

After a brief stay at Pitcairn Island, the captain and crew of the *Charles Dogget* prepared to take their leave. The grateful islanders presented Driver with a soup porringer cast from one of the HMS *Bounty's* pump boxes—which Driver's brother later used for heating shaving cream—and a letter of appreciation. Both the porringer and the letter eventually ended up in the Peabody Essex Museum.

After his final voyage, Driver retired to Nashville, Tennessee, where he lived with his daughter and her family. On special occasions, he would proudly display "Old Glory" in the window. But as the Civil War grew closer, the captain wisely decided to keep his flag hidden.

Driver's Confederate neighbors grew to hate both the flag and its owner. Throughout the war they frequently ransacked his home hoping to find and destroy Old Glory. Once they even tried to burn the house down.

Finally in February 1862 Union troops captured Nashville. When William Driver saw that the flag of the Sixth Ohio Regiment was flying over the capital building but that the American flag was absent, he knew it was time to remove his sacred banner from its hiding place. Ripping open the seams of the comforter that kept him warm on winter nights, William Driver extracted his flag. Soon Old Glory was seen flying over Nashville.

Five months before his death, William Driver sent his

As sales of the Gibralter grew, the Spencers acquired a cart and a shaggy gray pony to pull it. Eventually Gibralters found their way to the farthest corners of the globe on Salem vessels. It has been said that no Salem ship would dare leave port without a supply.

beloved ensign to a niece, Caroline Buswell, who donated it to the Essex Institute in Salem. After a few years it was sent on to its present home at the Smithsonian Institution.

The Gibralter

Another lasting treasure from Salem's maritime trade era is the Gibralter, a candy made famous throughout the world by the Spencers of Salem.

Mrs. Spencer and her son Thomas sailed from England sometime around 1806 and supposedly lost everything they owned in a shipwreck. Some say the year was 1826. The ambiguity surrounding the exact year is par for the course where the Spencers are concerned. There is much about them that can only be surmised.

The same can be said for the Spencers' famous confection. The candies were originally called Gibraltar Rocks, probably because of their hardness. Why and when the name was shortened and the spelling of *Gibralter* was changed is unknown.

The origin of the recipe for Gibralters is equally unclear. It has been written that it was given to Thomas Spencer by an Italian sailor who learned of it from the monks at a hilltop monastery in Abruzzi, Italy. Others say the recipe was brought to America, and ultimately to Spencer, from England by a Mr. Ashby who had learned of it from a British soldier who in turn discovered the candy while he was stationed in Egypt.

Whatever its source, the Gibralter recipe would be good to Mr. Spencer and his mother. A kindly citizen was said to have donated a barrel of sugar to the Spencers, and Thomas began making the tasty paper-wrapped lemon confection in a house at 56 Buffum Street in North Salem. His mother sold the candies on the stoop of the First Church in Town House Square. As sales grew, the Spencers acquired a cart and a shaggy gray pony to pull it.

Eventually Gibralters found their way to the farthest corners of the globe on Salem vessels. It has been said that no Salem ship would dare leave port without a supply.

When Mrs. Spencer died, Thomas had her body embalmed and placed in a metallic casket to preserve it. The reasons for his actions soon became clear. Not long after her death Thomas supposedly fell heir to a fortune back in England and moved—lock, stock, and mother's body—back to his native country.

What Thomas Spencer didn't take home with him was his thriving confection business. That was sold around 1830 to a Mr. John Pepper, who continued making Gibralters on Buffum Street. Either he or the Spencers also began making peppermint and checkerberry-flavored Gibralters. In addition, Mr. Pepper made Salem's other popular sweet, the syrupy molasses-and-sugar Black Jacks.

Eleanor Putnam contrasts these two candies in *Old Salem*. The Gibralter, Putnam offers, "is the aristocrat of Salem confectionary," and although it is so "unutterably flinty-hearted that it is almost a libel upon the rock whose name it bears," it grows to be a great comfort and a cherished companion in old age.

The burnt-tasting Black Jack, on the other hand, has about it a "reckless and somewhat devil-may-carishness," opines Putnam. "It is preeminently the joy of the youthful. It satisfies young ambition."

Putnam concludes her chapter on Salem's two institutions with this thought: "Witch Hill may blow away; the East India Museum may be swallowed up in earth; Charter Street Burying Ground may go out to sea; but as long as a single house remains standing in Salem Village, so long will Black-Jack and Gibralter wisely reign, and retain their honorable place in the inmost hearts of the Salem people."

Today, more than a century and a half after they first appeared on the Salem scene, these two beloved candies are still made at Ye Olde Pepper Companie on Derby Street. The business is owned by descendants of George Burkinshaw, who went to work for John Pepper when Pepper bought the company in 1830.

Salem and the *Constitution*

ᏉᎧ

One Sunday during the War of 1812, the services of the Second Church were interrupted by the appearance of a parishioner at a window near the pew of James Brown. He was George Crowninshield, and he was bringing news that the *Constitution*, the pride of the American fleet, had been chased into Marblehead Harbor by two British cruisers.

The information was relayed to the pulpit where the Reverend William Bentley was holding forth. The minister promptly abandoned his sermon and shouted, "This is a time for action, not words. Let us go to do what we can to save the *Constitution* and may God be with us. Amen." With that he grabbed his hat and started out the door. His congregation followed.

But the *Constitution* was in good hands, thanks to the work of another of Bentley's parishioners. Joseph Perkins, the Salem Harbor pilot headquartered on Baker's Island, had seen the vessel's plight and rowed out to meet it. Perkins had guided the *Constitution* into Marblehead Harbor where it was anchored under the safety of the cannon at Fort Sewall.

Shortly before this incident a party had been given at Hamilton Hall on Chestnut Street in honor of the *Constitution*'s skipper, Commodore Bainbridge, and other officers of the U.S. Navy. The highlight of the event had been the unveiling of a model of the commodore's famous vessel. The model was equipped with miniature cannon that actually worked. At a given signal, the fuses were lit and the guns went off. Unfortunately, the blasts blew the rigging right off of the toy ship. The model was subsequently repaired by British prisoners being held on a nearby prison ship.

Hamilton Hall

Hamilton Hall was designed by Salem's great architect-carver Samuel McIntire.

McIntire came from a long line of housewrights and carpenters. Early in his career he caught the eye of Elias Derby and built or remodeled a number of homes for Salem's leading ship owner. McIntire also designed mansions for John Gardner, Jonathan Hodges, and other members of Salem's elite merchant class.

A group of wealthy Federalists hired McIntire to build an assembly hall on Chestnut Street in 1805. The hall, which was named for Alexander Hamilton, the nation's first Secretary of the Treasury, hosted assemblies, debutante balls, fairs, and classes in dance, art, and music. A gala was held in the second-floor assembly hall for the Marquis de Lafayette during the Frenchman's visit in 1824.

The first floor was occupied by John Remond, a caterer known for his turtle soup luncheons and a purveyor of provisions. At various times in the mid-twentieth century, the downstairs rooms housed an antique dealer, a women's dress shop, and a fabric shop.

Just opposite the hall on Chestnut Street stood the magnificent new South Church, also designed by Samuel McIntire and completed in 1805. The first minister of the parish, the crusty Dr. Hopkins, took a jaundiced view of the couples dancing across the way in Hamilton Hall. "Back to back, breast to breast," he is supposed to have snarled, "they are dancing their way into hell."

Dr. Hopkins's church burned to the ground just before Christmas in 1903. Couples are still tripping the light fantastic in Hamilton Hall.

The spinsters of Federal Street

Acccording to oral tradition, Samuel McIntire was also retained by the merchant Jerethmiel Peirce to design and build a three-story clapboard home for him on a lot overlooking the North River.

Peirce probably moved into his new mansion in 1783. He lived there for more than forty years until a series of economic reversals forced him to sell his house at auction in 1827. The high bidders were Peirce's friends, George and Martha Johonnet. Martha's will stipulated that after her death, ownership of the house would eventually revert to the Peirce heirs.

Thanks to the generosity of the Johonnets, Jerethmiel's daughter Betsy and son-in-law George Nichols reclaimed the house in 1840. With them came George's children by his first wife, who had passed away; she happened to be Betsy's sister Sally.

None of George Nichols's four daughters ever married, and later in life they became known as the "Aunties." In 1888 George's son John also took up residence in the Pierce mansion with his three unmarried daughters. They, too, remained single and were nicknamed the "Maidens." "Cupid," one of the spinsters once noted, "passed by this house with drooping wings and averted eyes."

George Nichols's daughter Sarah was a bit of a character. She made it a point to take a long walk every day and to record her mileage. In her lifetime the spinster covered 150,000 miles, most of them on the streets of Salem. In bad weather Sarah got her exercise pacing in the barn behind her home.

Andrew Jackson's visit to Salem

One of the more bizarre stories relating to an important visitor to Salem involves President Andrew Jackson's stop in town in 1833 on his grand tour of New England.

Jackson, being a Democrat and a true man of the people, was despised by many in the elite Whig party. Ten-year-old Caroline King's parents were among those who held the president in contempt and young Caroline had adopted her parents' sentiments.

The youngster and her friend Lucy Saltonstall were frequent visitors to the maritime and ethnology museum in the East India Marine Hall on Essex Street. In fact, they had come to view the museum as their own private domain. So when the two girls learned that Jackson had toured the museum with Vice President Van Buren, they were incensed.

The following day Caroline and Lucy headed to the East India Marine Hall to inspect the guest book. Sure enough, the signatures of Jackson and Van Buren were sprawled across the page for the preceding day. The girls promptly returned home to plot their strategy for undoing this frightful sacrilege.

Later they returned to the museum armed with a pair of scissors. When no one was looking, they removed part of the offending page and raced home. In a few minutes all that was left of the evidence was a few ashes.

The discovery of the missing signatures set off an ugly furor in the press and on the streets of Salem that lasted for weeks. Charges and countercharges were leveled by both Whigs and Democrats. Caroline and her friend somehow managed to keep their lips sealed. They finally revealed their terrible secret to close family members seventy years later.

The museum's guest book for 1833 now bears a written notation: "Here on this page were once the signatures of Andrew Jackson and Martin Van Buren—Mutilated by some person or persons unknown."

Mobile homes

A common sight in nineteenth-century Salem was a house being dragged down a city street by oxen on its way to a new location.

In 1818 William Roberts, a mason who would later build the East India Marine Hall, St. Peter's Church, and the Salem train depot, bought a house at the corner of Mall Street opposite Salem Common. Roberts then set out to move the house to a lot on the southwest corner of the intersection of Federal Street and Federal Street Court which he had purchased from the pastor of the Roman Catholic Society of Boston, John Cheverus.

Smaller sections of the house were easily transported across town, but the main body of the massive three-story building went reluctantly. Writing in his journal on May 20, 1818, Salem diarist William Bentley noted that town residents were "amused, not to say affronted" by the proceedings.

"The main house was dragged into the street," Bentley recounted, "and stood for a week. Yesterday it passed St. Peter's Church. The pumps on the street corner were removed and the cornerstone of the church, and after a long day's work, with a team of sixty oxen with proper drivers and with screws, chains and cables, I saw it turned. The operation did no honor to their judgement."

Perhaps this traffic-snarling incident was still in the minds of the Salem city councilors who balked at giving Caroline Emmerton permission to move the 1682 Hathaway Bakery building from the corner of Washington and Federal Streets to a site adjacent to the newly restored House of Seven Gables. Emmerton was finally able to convince the councilors that the bakery was of historic value, and she was given the green light to move it.

The building was transported in three sections along Bridge, Webb, and Derby Streets to its new home on Salem Harbor. In *The Chronicles of Three Old Houses,* Emmerton noted that "when each part of the house arrived it looked like the Birnam Woods, having torn off a great deal of foliage from the overarching elms on the way down."

One of the farthest moves of a historic Salem property involved the Stephen Phillips Memorial Trust House at 34 Chestnut Street. The Phillips House was once part of Nathaniel and Elizabeth (Derby) West's Oak Hill Farm, now the site of the North Shore Shopping Center. The couple divorced in 1806, and Elizabeth was awarded the farm. When she died in 1814, the property passed to her three daughters with the provision that none of the property could end up in Nathaniel's possession.

When the couple's daughter Sarah died in 1819, however, Nathaniel somehow inherited this structure, which was part of the estate. Shortly thereafter he had the house moved on wheels three miles to Chestnut Street and installed a central hallway and a full third floor. The home was bought by Stephen W. Phillips in 1913 and turned into a museum by the Phillips family in 1971 after the death of his son Stephen.

One house move had a tragic ending. On January 25, 1796, Nathaniel Richardson was crushed by a house he was moving down Daniels Street toward the harbor. Richardson, whose tannery on the eastern side of the Salem Common was the largest in Essex County, slipped and fell onto a pile of timbers just as the house slid off its cradle in his direction. Death was instantaneous.

The Grimshawe House and Elizabeth Peabody

CʃƆ

In 1835 a Salem dentist named Nathaniel Peabody bought a three-story home just east of the Burying Point on Charter Street.

Peabody and his wife Elizabeth had three daughters, Elizabeth, Mary, and Sophia. "Lizzie," the oldest of the sisters, was an educator and a cultural gadfly who was well known in Boston and Salem. Thanks to her, a number of soon-to-be-famous men came calling at the Peabodys' modest home.

Two such men were Nathaniel Hawthorne, a budding Salem author who would later give the Charter Street home its name when he used it as a setting in his stories "Dr. Grimshawe's Secret" and "Dolliver's Romance"; and the Boston educator Horace Mann. Nathaniel would marry Sophia Peabody in 1842. A year later her sister Mary wed Horace Mann, the first Massachusetts superintendent of schools.

Elizabeth, the "introducer," never married but became famous as a feminist, educator, bookstore owner, and author. She ran two schools of her own and worked at Bronson Alcott's controversial Temple School in Boston. She later opened the nation's first kindergarten on Beacon Hill in 1861, and she was largely responsible for the spread of the kindergarten movement in America.

Ms. Peabody later became one of America's first female publishers. Using the name E. P. Peabody to disguise her gender, she printed antislavery tracts, children's books by Nathaniel Hawthorne, and the *Dial*, the journal of the transcendentalists who gathered at her Boston bookstore. She also provided a forum for the early female lecturer Margaret Fuller.

Elizabeth's writings reflect her connections to important men of the times: *Reminiscences of Rev. William Ellery Channing*, *Record of a School* (about Alcott's Temple School), and *A Last Evening with Allston* (about painter Washington Allston).

After her death in 1894, Lizzie's friends opened the Elizabeth Peabody House, a combination social service agency and kindergarten, in Boston to carry on her work.

Nathaniel Hawthorne loses a job and gains fame

Salem's most famous native son is the author of *The Scarlet Letter* and *The House of the Seven Gables*.

Some of the more poignant stories about Nathaniel Hawthorne relate to the dark period following his ouster by local Whigs from his job at the Salem Custom House, which he held for nearly twenty-seven months.

The day he lost his job Hawthorne was both humiliated by the firing and worried about how he would support his wife and two children. When he arrived home early from work at his Mall Street home, Sophia was delighted and surprised to see him.

According to their son Julian, upon learning that Nathaniel had been fired, Sophia replied, "Oh then, you can write your book!" When Nathaniel reminded his wife that they had to eat, she led her husband to her desk and opened the drawer. There lay a pile of gold coins that, unbeknownst to him, she had saved from his salary and the sale of her artwork.

And so Hawthorne, already the author of many popular short stories and sketches, was able to begin "his book." As the months slipped by and Sophia's secret cache dwindled, help came from an unexpected source. At the Salem Post Office one January day in 1850 Hawthorne opened a letter from his friend George Hillard. Enclosed was a check for $500 collected from anonymous friends for "the debt we owe you for what you have done for American literature."

Hawthorne wrote back to Hillard that the gesture had brought "water to my eyes; so that I was glad of the sharply cold west wind that blew into them as I came homeward, and gave them an excuse for being red and bleared."

By early February, Hawthorne had finished *The Scarlet Letter*. His first inkling of its power came from his wife. Hawthorne reported to a friend that after listening to his reading of the book's final chapter, Sophia "went to bed with a grievous headache—which I look upon as a triumphant success!"

Sometime in November or December 1849 Hawthorne received a visit from James Fields of the Boston publishing house of Ticknor, Reed and Fields. The publisher, who had unsuccessfully lobbied various politicians to let Hawthorne keep his job at the Custom House, was sure the author had been writing. During their visit Fields offered to print two thousand copies of whatever work Hawthorne had completed.

Hawthorne led Fields to believe that ever since his firing he had not been in a suitable frame of mind to write. Fields later recalled, "I then caught sight of a bureau or set of drawers near where we were sitting; and immediately it occurred to me that hidden away somewhere in that article of furniture was a story or stories by the author of *Twice-Told Tales* and I became so positive of it that I charged him vehemently with the fact."

Hawthorne denied that any such thing existed, and a frustrated Fields prepared to leave to catch a train back to Boston. As the publisher headed down the stairs, Hawthorne stopped him. He then disappeared back into his house and returned with a manuscript. This he gave to Fields saying, "How in Heaven's name did you know this thing was there?"

Fields's intuition and persistence would pay handsome dividends. The manuscript contained most of the story of *The Scarlet Letter*. The book, when published in its entirety by Ticknor, Reed and Fields a few months later, would be both financially and critically successful.

The Hawthornes moved to Lenox in June 1850. Just before their departure Nathaniel was in Boston when he ran into Horace Conolly, the adopted son of his cousin Susan Ingersoll. The two men spent a few hours drinking and conversing, despite Hawthorne's firm belief that Conolly had played a major role in his firing from the Custom House. Ironically, Conolly had written Hawthorne asking for help in securing for himself the position Hawthorne had just lost.

The author was incredulous at the irony of the situation. He wrote Conolly that their meeting in Boston was "almost too incredible to be put into a romance. . . . I don't reckon you among my enemies nor ever have. You are kind of a pet serpent, and must be allowed to bite now and then, that being the nature of the critter."

Patrick Gilmore and the Salem Brass Band

Oone of the greatest sources of civic pride in mid-nineteenth-century Salem was the Salem Brass Band, a military band attached to the Salem Light Infantry. The outfit had been organized in 1837 and was a familiar sight at militia drills, parades, and other public gatherings.

In December 1854 the band offered its vacant bandleader position to a twenty-three-year-old native of County Galway,

Ireland, by the name of Patrick Sarsfield Gilmore. The salary was $1,000 a year plus all the income the bandleader could generate from band activities. Gilmore accepted the offer and took the reins of the Salem band the following month. The choice of Gilmore was a stroke of good fortune for the Salem Brass Band and the Salem Light Infantry. The young bandleader proved to be a brilliant organizer and a creative genius.

Gilmore had left home at age nine to move to a British military town that was the home base of the British Militia Regimental Band. The youngster learned to play the fife, the one-keyed bugle, and the cornet. Before long he was also composing waltzes, polkas, and marches.

When he came of age for military service the lad joined the regimental band. Soon after he joined the unit in 1848 it was sent to Canada. From there the young musician made his way to Boston, where he organized both a minstrel group and a militia band. In 1854 Patrick Gilmore briefly led the prestigious Boston Brass Band before leaving to take over the Salem outfit.

Gilmore proceeded to work his magic in Salem just as he had done in Boston. In 1857 the Salem band's reputation earned it a highly sought-after invitation from the New England Guards, a militia company, to play at the inauguration of U.S. President James Buchanan.

The Salem Brass Band's performance in the nation's capital was praised by the Washington press, further enhancing the band's reputation as one of the nation's leading outfits. But the publicity also enraged Boston-area bands who had not been chosen to make the trip.

Their egos bruised, a group of Bostonians decided to ambush Gilmore's group at the Boston train depot when the Salem band returned from Washington. The plan was to destroy the Salem musicians' instruments and knock their lips out of service. Fortunately for the unsuspecting Salem band members, they caught an earlier train home and missed their surprise rendezvous with their envious rivals.

Through the music grapevine Gilmore later learned of the failed plot. Before the band's next trip to Boston the young bandleader took appropriate steps to protect his men. He recruited a squad of Salem goons, all armed with blackjacks and brass knuckles, to accompany his musicians to Boston.

As expected, Gilmore's band members were set upon by a hostile crowd of Bostonians immediately upon disembarking from the train. The Salem thugs, lurking in the background, raced down the train platform and did what they were brought along to do. The Boston "musician toughs" received a substantial dose of their own medicine.

But the people of Boston would have the last word. In a classic example of "if you can't beat 'em, join 'em," Gilmore was lured away from Salem to take over the famous Boston Brigade Band, which he would reorganize and then lead for three decades.

Within a few years Patrick S. Gilmore's Boston Brigade Band was arguably the finest military band in the nation, and its leader was staking out his reputation as a peer of the brilliant John Philip Sousa.

"Federal Street"

❦

Another important figure in the nineteenth-century Salem music scene was the remarkable Henry Kemble Oliver. In addition to serving as mayor of Lawrence, Massachusetts, for two years and mayor of Salem for four, he was treasurer of Massachusetts, adjutant general of the Massachusetts Militia, head of the Massachusetts Bureau of Labor Statistics, and agent for a Lawrence cotton mill. Henry also played a dozen instruments and was an organist at area churches. He organized or ran a number of Salem music societies.

Henry Kemble Oliver was a serious composer of church

music. One of his best-known compositions, "Federal Street," can be found in many Protestant hymnals. Originally Oliver had planned to name the hymn after his wife, but a friend suggested that such a title would be inappropriate for a piece of religious music. The composer relented and renamed the tune after the Salem street on which he lived.

From then on, even after Oliver's death, the Salem Cadet Band stopped in front of his home at 138 Federal Street during the Memorial Day parade to play "Federal Street."

The train comes to Salem

ᏨᎶ

Salem's first train depot, which preceded the Gothic granite structure that many local inhabitants remember, was built on a wharf over the South River soon after the Eastern Railroad was extended to Salem in 1838. The river at the time still flowed inland along the line of present-day New Derby Street, filled what is now Riley Plaza, and continued on along what are now Jefferson Avenue and Canal Street to South Salem. Most of the river was filled in by the mid-1880s.

The wooden depot was capped by a cupola and a bell that was rung to announce arriving trains. The bell-ringer was "Corporal" Pitman, one of Salem's more colorful citizens. Pitman once remarked that he could "always tell when any one else was ringing that bell, by the sound."

On one occasion the train from Boston was late in arriving. Word filtered into Salem that the cause of the delay was a fire in Lynn. Someone asked William Oliver, the deputy collector at the Salem Custom House and another town character, the location of the fire. "I am told that it is in Lynn; I guess I will step over and see," Oliver said.

Henceforth Oliver was known as "Old step over to Lynn."

The Eastern Railroad, later the Boston and Maine, was a

major contributor to the construction of the Salem Normal School, the state's second public institution of higher education, built in 1854. The railroad chipped in $2,000 of the total construction cost of $13,500.

The railroad's investment would prove a wise one. The Salem train depot was located two short blocks from the school, and the train became the primary mode of transportation for the growing student population.

One of the city's more embarrassing moments occurred when the Prince of Wales, later King Edward VII, was scheduled to make a brief stop in Salem on October 20, 1860, on his train tour of the eastern United States.

A platform for local dignitaries was erected at the southern end of the old Washington Street train tunnel. The length of the train was calculated and a line was drawn on the wall of the tunnel to indicate where the engineer should stop so that His Highness's private car would end up opposite the receiving platform.

On the day of the Prince's visit, unbeknownst to Salem officials, an extra car had been added to the train in Boston. When the engineer stopped at the designated spot, the prince's car was a rod away from the dignitaries' platform. City officials frantically signaled to the engineer to pull forward.

The engineer misinterpreted the signal. Thinking the event had been scrapped, he proceeded north through the tunnel toward Beverly with Mayor Stephen Webb and other city officials, dressed in formal attire, in hot pursuit.

Webb finally caught up with the train and managed to exchange formalities with His Highness. Some of the other local dignitaries, perhaps out of sheer embarrassment, continued through the tunnel to the other end and went home.

Stephen Webb, mayor

⁂

Stephen Webb was Salem's fourth chief executive, serving three one-year terms as mayor between 1841 and 1843. He was subsequently reelected to the corner office three more times in 1860–62.

Between stints as Salem's mayor, Webb served a single term as mayor of San Francisco in 1854 at the height of the wild and woolly California Gold Rush. He later gave a lecture at the Salem Lyceum on the vigilance committees that managed to bring order to the dangerous San Francisco streets when legal authorities could not.

After the great San Francisco earthquake in 1906, the people of Salem sent $4,000 to that city's relief fund in memory of Stephen Webb. The citizens of San Francisco reciprocated after the Salem fire of 1914.

A very special flower

⁂

In the early 1850s the Salem horticulturist John Fiske Allen acquired an Amazon lily from a Philadelphia grower. The giant lily stood six feet tall and was named the Victoria Regia for the reigning monarch of England.

Allen, who grew over three hundred species of grapes, kept the lily in his greenhouse at 31 Chestnut Street. According to *Old Salem Gardens,* published by the Salem Garden Club in 1946, the plant's leaves grew at the rate of half an inch an hour. Some measured six feet in diameter and were strong enough for a child to stand on. The blossoms alone measured a foot and a half in diameter and gave off a pineapple scent. The lily grew so large that the greenhouse had to be enlarged. Jones Very, Salem's transcendentalist poet, honored the Victoria Regia in verse:

> With reverence on thy beauty would I gaze,
> Inhale the fragrance, and admire thy Leaf,
> Whose wondrous size, and structure claim our praise
> Surpassing our conception and belief.

The first Filene's

In 1856 a young German immigrant opened his first dry goods store in the Bowker Block at 144-156 Essex Street. His name was William Filene, and he would go on to become one of New England's foremost retailers.

Filene and his family lived for a few years on nearby Brown Street before moving to New York City's Fifth Avenue. William's son Edward later recalled that relocating from "contracting, close-packed Salem to New York was like moving to the country." The Salem store was eventually closed in 1864.

Luis Emilio and the "Brave Black Regiment"

Shortly after shots were fired on Fort Sumter in April 1861, nineteen members of the Union Drill Club in Salem enlisted in the Massachusetts Twenty-third Volunteer Regiment.

One of the nineteen recruits was sixteen-year-old Luis Emilio, the son of a Spanish immigrant and a respected musician. Emilio served with distinction in the South Carolina campaign and was quickly promoted to sergeant.

In March 1863, Luis was transferred to the newly organized Fifty-fourth Massachusetts Volunteer Regiment commanded by Colonel Robert Gould Shaw. This regiment consisted of six hundred free black soldiers serving under white officers. Four months later, Emilio, now a captain, marched with his new outfit against Fort Wagner near Charleston, South Carolina.

The assault was poorly planned, and as a result 272 of the 621 members of the Fifty-fourth Regiment were killed, captured, or wounded. Luis Emilio was the highest-ranking officer to survive and briefly took over the regimental command.

In April 1865, less than a week before General Robert E. Lee surrendered the Confederate Army, Emilio was discharged. He subsequently married and moved to New York City, where he spent most of the rest of his life.

Years later Luis interviewed many of the surviving members of the Fifty-fourth Regiment and put their collective memories on paper. In 1891 those memories were published under the title *A Brave Black Regiment.* Although much else has been written on this famous groundbreaking outfit, Emilio's book remains the definitive work. Nearly a century later, the book served as the basis for Tri-Star Pictures' movie *Glory.*

Sarah Parker Remond, abolitionist

೭ಾ

One of the unsung heroes of the Civil War, and one of Salem's most famous abolitionists, was Sarah Parker Remond.

Sarah was one of eight children of John Remond, an African-American native of Curaçao who moved to Salem in 1798 and established himself as a caterer and purveyor of exotic groceries in Hamilton Hall on Chestnut Street.

John and his son Charles were active members of the Massachusetts Anti-Slavery Committee. Sarah grew up attending abolitionist lectures and rallies and eventually joined the Salem Female Anti-Slavery Society. She was also inspired by William Lloyd Garrison and other important abolitionists who visited the Remond home.

In 1856 Sarah was chosen by the American Anti-Slavery Society to participate in a lecture tour of western New York State, Pennsylvania, Ohio, Massachusetts, Michigan, and Canada. She was the only African-American woman in the group, which also included noted abolitionists Wendell Phillips, Susan B. Anthony, and Sarah's now-famous brother Charles. One of the final stops on the tour was the landmark National Woman's Rights Conference in New York City in 1858.

By January 1859 Sarah was in England, where she would remain until the end of the American Civil War, spreading her message that because all humans are God's creatures, enslaving others is evil.

Women lecturers, especially women of color, were a rarity in the British Isles, and Remond's brilliant oratory and devoutly moral antislavery message made her highly sought after as a speaker. Her talks attracted as many as two thousand people at a time, most of them white, and often inspired important resolutions, press articles, financial contributions, and other types of support for the American abolitionist movement.

By mobilizing support for her antislavery message from the general population, Sarah helped keep the natural relationship between the powerful British textile interests and the cotton growers in the Confederate states from developing into English military and diplomatic support for the South.

Sarah Remond returned to America briefly after the Civil War but was back in England by 1866. Soon after that she moved to Florence, Italy, where she trained as a doctor of medicine at a local hospital. She married a man named Pintor, exactly when is not known, and lived and practiced medicine in Florence until her death in 1894.

Lieutenant Maury's fall from grace

❧

In 1848 Lt. Matthew Fontaine Maury, who had recently charted the portion of the Atlantic Ocean that lies between New York and the equator, was honored by both the Salem and the East India Marine Societies. Henceforth a photograph of the explorer would be proudly displayed in the headquarters of both societies. Maury was further rewarded with the first honorary membership ever bestowed by Salem's prestigious East India Marine Society.

But the young man's Salem admirers quickly turned on him when Maury allied himself with the Confederacy in the Civil War. In July 1861 the East India Marine Society voted to rescind his membership, deeming him no longer worthy of the honor. It was further voted that his photograph be removed from display in the East India Marine Hall and "stored in some obscure corner of the building."

The members of the Salem Marine Society voted to leave Lieutenant Maury's portrait in place but decreed that from that time forward it be "hung head down."

The Salem Lyceum

❧

Daniel Webster, John Quincy Adams, Ralph Waldo Emerson, and Henry David Thoreau were some of the most important figures of their times, and they all appeared at the Lyceum Hall in Salem.

The Salem Lyceum Society was organized in 1830 for the purpose of providing "mutual education and rational entertainment" for its members and the general public. Over the next sixty years the society would sponsor approximately one thousand lectures on topics relating to history, biography, science, religion, and other disciplines, as well as musical and theatrical performances.

Emerson spoke there nearly three dozen times, while Daniel Webster was paid the highest fee, one hundred dollars. Nathaniel Hawthorne never appeared onstage at the Church Street hall, but he served as the society's corresponding secretary during his last year in Salem. Among the speakers he engaged were his brother-in-law Horace Mann and his famous publisher James Fields.

Only half a dozen women were numbered among the presenters. The best known was the noted British actress Fanny Kemble, who gave a reading from *A Midsummer Night's Dream* in 1850. Another woman speaker bore the fascinating name Laura F. Dainty.

The lectures often filled the five-hundred-seat amphitheater and had to be repeated the following night. The Congregationalists came one evening, their rivals the Universalists the other. Women were allowed to attend but were supposed to be "introduced," or chaperoned, by a man.

In a talk entitled "Reminiscences of Salem Sixty or Seventy Years Ago" before the Salem Rotary Club in 1952, and later published in the Essex Institute Historical Collections, Roger Poor recalled a Dr. Daniels who appeared at the Lyceum as part of a vaudeville show. "Daniels's specialty," said Poor, "was extracting teeth without pain, right on stage, no charge for the operation." According to one of Poor's schoolmates who allowed Dr. Daniels to yank one of his teeth, the procedure was done so quickly there was hardly any pain at all.

Demonstrating the telephone

✧

The overflow crowd at the Lyceum Hall in Salem was growing restless. The evening's program, one in a series sponsored by the Essex Institute, should have started twenty minutes earlier. Some of the five hundred paying customers had begun stamping their feet and rapping their canes on the hard wooden floor.

Suddenly the stage door opened and out strode a tall bearded man bearing a rectangular wooden box. The expectant crowd grew silent. After a brief introduction, he stepped to the front of the stage and began his presentation.

From the outset it was clear that the speaker was no stranger to the stage. Indeed, Alexander Graham Bell was a trained voice physiologist who since the age of sixteen had been demonstrating his father's "Visible Speech" method of teaching the hearing impaired to speak. Professor Bell was also an inventor. And on this night, February 12, 1877, he was to demonstrate his telephone apparatus to the public for the first time.

Bell began with a tribute to Salem's own Charles Grafton Page, whose experiments in sending musical sounds by electric currents in the 1830s had pioneered the field of telephony. Bell went on to describe briefly his own experiments and the workings of his new invention. Then he used the telephone to instruct his assistant Thomas Watson, who was stationed in their Exeter Street laboratory in Boston, to send an interrupted current followed by the alphabet in Morse code. The crowd was thrilled by the sounds coming through the telephone receiver on the stage, which could be heard even in the back of the hall thirty-five feet away.

Watson then activated a telephonic organ that played "America," "Yankee Doodle," and "Auld Lang Syne." The music could be heard in all corners of the hall. After making a few complimentary remarks about Watson, Bell asked his assistant to sing

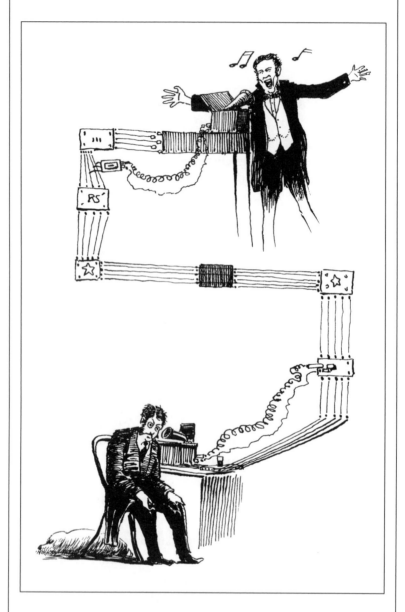

After making a few complimentary remarks about his assistant, Thomas Watson, Alexander Graham Bell asked him to sing "Auld Lang Syne."

"Auld Lang Syne." Watson obliged, albeit reluctantly, and then spoke directly to the audience:

"Ladies and Gentlemen—it gives me great pleasure to be able to address you this evening although I am in Boston and you are in Salem." His comments, clear as a bell, brought down the house.

Selected members of the audience were invited onstage to speak into Bell's marvelous invention. A Salem newspaper would later report that among those lucky few were "Rev. Dr. Bolles, Rev. Mr. Atwood, Professor Gage, Gen. Cogswell, a gentleman from Japan, and a lady (Mrs. Loring)." Watson answered their questions about that day's election results, the weather in Boston, and the status of the Boston and Maine Railroad strike. He then concluded with a rendition of "Hold the Fort."

Bell ended the program by briefly outlining potential commercial uses for his new invention. The applause from the audience was loud and long. Getting the public to leave the premises proved difficult; most wanted a closer look at the magic wooden box on the stage. Finally the gas lamps were dimmed, and the hall was cleared.

But the evening was not yet over. An officer of the Essex Institute used the telephone to thank Thomas Watson, who was born and raised in Salem, for his part in the program. Votes of thanks were also relayed to the Atlantic and Pacific Telegraph Company for the use of their wires and the services of their operator, Miss Molloy.

The telephone at Salem was then turned over to Henry Batchelder, a friend of Watson and a stringer for the *Boston Globe*. Batchelder used the device to dictate his account of what had just transpired at the Lyceum to a *Globe* reporter, A. B. Fletcher, who was with Watson in Boston. This was the first time Bell's new invention had been used to transmit a news story.

The accounts of Professor Bell's demonstration that appeared in the *Boston Globe* and other local papers generated even more interest in the telephone. The mayor of Salem and a group of leading citizens invited Bell to repeat his performance on February 23. This time the proceeds from the evening went to the inventor.

This second demonstration also drew a capacity crowd and proceeded almost as smoothly as the first. For his efforts, Bell collected $149. Of this amount he spent $85 to have a silver model of the telephone made for Mabel Hubbard, soon to become Mrs. Bell.

The second demonstration inspired a member of the audience, Salem's transcendental poet Jones Very, to pen a sonnet in celebration of Bell's invention. "The Telephone" begins:

> The marvel of our age, the Telephone!
> What is the Telephone, do you enquire?
> The marvel of our time, before unknown,
> The human voice speaks through the electric wire.

The impact of the Salem lectures on the future of the Bell Patent Association, which included Bell, Watson, and Bell's financial backers, Gardiner Hubbard and Thomas Sanders, would transcend poetry and publicity. Just a month before the Lyceum talks, Hubbard and Sanders had offered to sell all of Bell's patents to the Western Union Telegraph Company for $100,000. The men sorely needed a return on their substantial investment, and Bell needed money so that he could marry Hubbard's daughter. Thomas Watson was eagerly anticipating the $10,000 that would accrue to him after the sale went through.

Western Union rejected the offer, and it appeared that the Patent Association would be forced to manufacture and begin selling telephones just to generate cash. But the success of the Salem lectures gave the men another idea. Bell hired an agent and went on the road demonstrating the telephone in Boston, Providence, New York, and other eastern cities. The income from these lectures bought the company time to implement its original plan to develop a complete telephone service system that would be leased rather than sold.

The financial benefit of this strategy to the principals in the Bell Patent Association was beyond anyone's dreams. In his autobiography, *Exploring Life,* Thomas Watson claims that the Bell patents that Western Union refused to buy for $100,000 could not have been purchased two years later for $25,000,000.

Watson sees a psychic

Thomas Watson, like many Salemites of later generations, was drawn to the world of psychic phenomena. In *Exploring Life* Watson recounts childhood seances during which his friend George Phillips acted as medium. Their successful experiments with moving tables and slate writing (which lasted until George lost his powers as a medium) made Watson a firm believer in spiritualism.

Watson maintained a lifelong interest in psychic phenomena and was a member of the Society of Psychic Research. He was also a firm believer in reincarnation. His open-mindedness in such matters led him to seek assistance from a Boston psychic when he and Alexander Graham Bell reached an impasse in the development of Bell's new telephone.

The results? "She gave me such rubbish I never afterwards tried to get the spirits to give the telephone a boost," noted Watson. "I went back to the books of the Public Library as a more certain source of inspiration."

Moses Farmer

❧

Another famous American inventor with Salem ties was Moses Farmer, a great nineteenth-century electrician who served as a consultant to Alexander Graham Bell in matters of electricity.

Farmer moved to Salem in 1849 from New Hampshire, where he and his brother had invented and built a two-car electric train. Moses would later become famous as the inventor of a fire alarm system installed in buildings throughout the Boston area and later sold nationally.

In July 1859, twenty years before Thomas Edison "invented" the electric light, Farmer illuminated his Salem home at 11 Pearl Street with battery-powered electric incandescent lights. This was the first demonstration of electric lighting in America.

But all of the electrician's achievements paled in comparison with "the one that got away." After he read Bell's description of the telephone for the first time, Farmer told Thomas Watson that he was unable to sleep for a week because he was so mad at himself.

"Watson," Farmer grumbled, "that thing has flaunted itself in my face a dozen times during the last ten years and every time I was too blind to see it."

The leather strike of 1886

❧

In the first half of the nineteenth century, Salem gradually evolved from a maritime community to a center of industry. Leather, shoe, and cotton factories replaced the decks of East Indiamen as the new workplaces.

With the factories came the immigrants. The first to arrive in Salem were the Irish, in the 1830s. Most of them were leather workers looking for jobs in Salem's booming leather industry.

Around 1800 that industry had settled in Blubber Hollow near the banks of the North River. It continued to grow for another fifty years. By 1886 almost a thousand workers were working in tanning and currying shops located primarily on Boston, Goodhue, Grove, and Mason Streets.

Leather work was dangerous work. Many men lost fingers on the treacherous splitting machines. Other workers suffered broken arms or had their spines snapped after being dragged into machines that had latched onto their aprons.

The workweek was long—sixty-six hours—and in the decades after the Civil War, the work was much less financially rewarding than the leather workers thought reasonable. The decrease in wages could be partly explained by a general downturn in the industry. The rest the local workers blamed on greedy employers. In 1885 the Knights of Labor, a growing national union, organized local leather workers and used the threat of a strike to gain additional wages for them.

In early July 1886 the local Knights of Labor leadership presented shop owners with other demands, including a fifty-nine-hour workweek and a new pay scale that would provide extra compensation for the more dangerous jobs.

The owners of the Salem leather shops, a cohesive group known as "The Senate," met with their Peabody counterparts on July 9 and decided to reject the union's demands. Three days later the owners posted a resolution in their factories stating that in the future they would "employ only such men as will bargain individually with us and agree to take no part in any strike whatsoever." The resolution also emphatically stated that the owners were "determined to run our business without any dictation."

Fifteen hundred leather workers responded by walking off their jobs in Salem and Peabody. Worried owners donned aprons and helped each other finish processing hides that would otherwise be lost. Sons and other family members were recalled from company stores and offices in Boston to help.

Arrangements were quickly made to import leather workers from Maine and the Maritime Provinces in Canada. With their help and that of the local workers who had rejected the Knights of Labor, the owners were able to resume operation.

Angry strikers went on the offensive. A dummy appeared in front of one factory bearing a placard reading SCABS TO LET. Vehicles carrying imported workers were stoned, and nonunion workers were frequently attacked when caught alone by strikers.

The violence escalated in early August. Mobs of strikers attacked boarding houses in Peabody and Salem where the nonunion workers were staying. The police had to be called in to restore order. Police patrols were quickly established in the neighborhoods where the nonunion workers lived or worked. For the rest of August, Salem police officers had to live at the station when not on duty.

Eventually, public opinion began turning against the strikers. The *Salem Evening News* took to calling the strikers "unbridled hooligans," "tormentors," and worse. The Catholic Archdiocese of Boston condemned the strike and excommunicated the Catholic members of The Knights of Labor.

The leather shop owners had the upper hand throughout the strike. Although some of the imported workers were scared off, they were quickly replaced by others and joined by defectors from the ranks of the striking workers. The owners also had large inventories of finished leather on hand at the beginning of the work stoppage and thus were guaranteed a steady income.

The workers, on the other hand, had to survive on small stipends from the Knights of Labor. Most were having a difficult time keeping food on the table and the rent paid. When the owners flatly rejected the union's offers to settle the strike in July and September, the union workers were disheartened.

The conflict finally came to a head on Thanksgiving Day.

Early in the afternoon two nonunion workers were surrounded and badly beaten by a mob of two hundred strikers on Boston Street. The two men were rescued by police, but the unruly gang soon swelled to five hundred men. Many of them were drunk.

Later in the day the mob surrounded a trolley car owned by the Danvers and Salem Railroad. All the passengers were told to get off, except four nonunion workers. Three of them were severely beaten and had to be taken to the hospital. The hostile crowd then proceeded to smash all the windows in the trolley.

These violent acts were more than many striking workers could tolerate, and on November 29 those who could returned to work. Many of the striking workers found jobs hard to come by because the factory owners had retained the nonunion workers.

Most observers agreed afterward that the strike had been ill-timed because it provided tannery owners in other parts of the country with an opportunity to capture a piece of the lucrative New England leather market. As a result, many of Salem's smaller leather shops went out of business in the decade that followed.

Alvah and Aaron

෬

The leather shop owners didn't always get the upper hand as they did in the 1886 strike. Leather manufacturer Alvah Evans came upon Aaron Young, who worked for Salem's street department, as Young was repairing wooden planking on the North Bridge.

"Aaron, it would be a good plan for the city to build an iron bridge here. It would save considerable money in the long run," Evans said.

Young's response brought a quick end to the conversation: "Yes, so it would, and if people could wear iron shoes instead of leather shoes, they too would save considerable money in the long run."

Salem Willows

ℰℭ

For many local residents, one of the most reliable signs that spring has arrived is their first box of popcorn, chop suey sandwich, or game of Skee-Ball at Salem Willows.

Salem Willows Park is truly one of the city's treasures. The thirty-five-acre waterfront site, once home to a contagious disease hospital, was designated a city park in 1858 and is named for the original white willow trees that were planted on the land around 1800.

Like its counterparts in Revere, Nantasket, and Gloucester, the birth of the Salem Willows amusement park was linked to an emerging local transportation system. In 1877 the Naumkeag Street Railway Company began running horse-drawn trolleys to Salem Willows, already a popular seaside gathering spot. The company also started acquiring land for a planned amusement park.

That park opened for business on June 10, 1880, and was an immediate hit with the public. A daily column in the *Salem Evening News* kept readers abreast of happenings at the seaside park and reported that the Willows received as many as ten thousand visitors in a single day. Many arrived on the Naumkeag Street Railway Company trolleys, which ran every fifteen minutes from downtown Salem.

One of the major attractions on "the line" (as the new commercial strip was known) was the Willows Pavilion. This rather unusual-looking structure boasted a roller-skating rink, complete with a live orchestra, on the street level and a three-hundred-seat restaurant on the second floor. A rear tower in the pavilion housed a camera obscura, a novel apparatus that projected scenes from as far away as Beverly and Marblehead onto a white table in an otherwise dark room.

Just opposite the pavilion was the Willows Park Theatre. Early events at this popular open-air venue were organized by promoter John S. Moulton and included concerts by Moulton's own opera company. The always popular Salem Cadet Band, led by the irrepressible Frenchman and Juniper Point resident Jean Missud, gave regularly scheduled performances. On Sundays the band was restricted to programs of sacred music.

Thrill seekers gravitated toward the water chute at the intersection of Fort and Columbus Avenues. Patrons were hauled up to the top of a tall slide in small "boats" and then sped down a long track into a pool of water below. The less adventurous could enjoy a harbor cruise on the steamboat *Three Brothers,* ride the new carousel, or test their marksmanship at the shooting gallery.

The carousel was located in the building at the end of the line that now houses Hobbes' Restaurant. The merry-go-round was powered by a mule who was hitched to a central post in the basement. The ride lasted only as long as the mule was willing to walk his prescribed circular route.

Visitors looking for a "shore dinner" at the Willows could drop in at Judge Chase's Willow House (opened in 1874) or Ebsen's on what would later become known as Restaurant Row. Other eateries appeared along the line. The most popular, until it was destroyed by fire, was Downing's, which stood on the site now occupied by the Hobbes family's popcorn and ice cream stand.

Everett Hobbes and Wilbur Eaton first began selling popcorn and other products at the Willows in the mid-1880s at a concession in the pavilion. In 1897 the partners founded the National Popcorn Company and opened a plant in Lynn on Western Avenue. At that same time, the men acquired the carousel building at the Willows, where they sold popcorn, taffy, and other summer delights. In 1906 they introduced a new product, the ice cream cone, to the American public.

Joseph Brown carved all of his carousel's horses, camels, lions, and other animals in his studio on what is now Bay View Avenue.

By the turn of the century the Willows amusement park was in full flower. From his tiny stand on the water side of Hobbes and Eaton, Patrick Kenneally hawked Spanish double-jointed peanuts to curious visitors. The sightless vendor was the first in the country to import this exotic item and was long remembered for his sales cry: "They're double-jointed Spanish peanuts all the way from Barcelona. Try 'em before you buy 'em."

At the other end of the line, at the corner of Harbor View (now Bay View) Avenue, stood Professor Kenerson's dance hall. The ballroom was a popular weekend destination and often attracted crowds in excess of fifteen hundred people on weekend nights.

Food establishments, a police station, and a post office (located in Downing's Restaurant) could all be found on the strip between the casino and Kenneally's peanut stand. Other attractions along the line included a shooting gallery, a pool room, and a photographer. By 1900 J. C. B. Smith was operating a slot machine arcade at the Willows. Apparently earlier sanctions against games of chance had been lifted.

Opposite Fort Avenue from the casino, on a knoll most recently occupied by a Tilt-a-Whirl and roller coaster, stood John W. Gorman's Summer Theatre. Gorman offered a repertoire of vaudeville and other live performances on his open-air stage. He also promoted other events, including balloon ascensions, bonfires, and parachute jumps, at the Willows.

Adjacent to Gorman's theatre stood Brown's Flying Horses. Joseph Brown, a native of Bavaria and an expert woodcarver, emigrated to America in 1870 and settled in Salem. Soon after his arrival, Brown opened a new merry-go-round at the Salem Willows.

Brown carved all of the carousel's horses, camels, lions, and other animals in his studio on what is now Bay View Avenue. The horses' tails and manes were made of real hair. Some of the wooden steeds were named after popular race horses of the day.

Brown also carved the miniature village that stood in the center of the carousel. It took him twenty years to complete the tableaux, which included wooden houses, churches, trees, and even a circus parade.

The carousel was originally turned by Mr. Brown and later by a real horse. Eventually a steam-driven engine was employed to power the carousel on its five-minute, one-mile trip. The carousel was a fixture in the Willows for seventy years.

Brown's Flying Horses were a popular attraction until 1945 when Brown's son-in-law, who operated the business for nearly twenty years, passed away. The horses were eventually sold to Macy's Department Store and for a time were displayed in the chain's New York store at Christmas time.

Twentieth Century

In the summer of 1909 Arthur Howard started a second paper, the Gazette. *Now he could scream, in huge Hearstian headlines, that two of the three newspapers in Salem supported his candidacy for mayor.*

Harry Houdini comes to town

ভে

Harry Houdini, the great escape artist, stopped in Salem in 1906 for a three-day stage engagement at the Salem Theatre.

As usual, he impressed audiences with his escapes from straitjackets, an assortment of chains and handcuffs, and a locked barrel. Even a facsimile of an allegedly escape-proof German jail cell couldn't contain the great one.

To silence critics who believed his stage events were "fixed," Houdini allowed himself to be stripped, locked in three pairs of police handcuffs and two pairs of leg irons, and thrown in a cell in the Salem police station. His clothes were locked in a separate cell. Thirteen minutes later the illusionist strolled into the marshal's office through the outside door, completely dressed. But he wasn't alone. Shackled to Houdini's wrist, much to the chagrin of the embarrassed marshal, was another prisoner.

The saga of Arthur Howard

ভে

Certainly the most bizarre saga in the history of Salem politics was the successful 1909 mayoral candidacy of Arthur Howard, who had been a resident of Salem for only fourteen months.

Howard was born in New York City in 1869 and raised in that city's elegant Washington Square neighborhood. His father, Joseph, once described as "the dean of the jewelry trade in New York City" in the *New York Times,* sent Arthur to a private school with the sons of the powerful Huntington, Gould, and Rockefeller families.

Arthur left school at age fourteen and spent nearly twenty years working at his father's firm. He married Annie Legg when he was twenty-three, and the couple had one daughter. In 1906 the Howards moved to London where Arthur had established himself as a representative for American jewelry firms. This new venture would be short-lived because Howard lost both his business and his life savings in the American economic collapse of 1907.

Arthur left his wife and daughter in Europe and returned home to begin picking up the pieces. Soon after his arrival in New York, he learned of the death of his cousin Joseph Howard, Jr., whose "Howard Letters" column appeared regularly in the *Boston Globe*. Arthur traveled to Boston in the hopes of taking over Joseph's column, but the *Globe* had other plans for the column. The thirty-eight-year-old Howard then decided to start his own paper in nearby Salem, where many of his ancestors had lived. Although he knew nothing about publishing newspapers, Arthur had written more than a dozen books. His literary output included *Grandmother's Cookbook, The XYZ of Wall Street,* and *Shakespeare for the Unsophisticated.* Some of his books had sold as many as 40,000 copies.

On October 24, 1908, Howard published the first issue of the *Salem Morning Dispatch* with the help of an out-of-work Boston printer named Ralph Lee. Shortly afterward, Howard bought a secondhand printing press on credit and some odd lots of type. He then set up shop in a rented paint shed on Central Street in Salem.

Howard's *Dispatch* was a long shot to survive. Because of the power of the *Salem Evening News,* it was nearly impossible for Howard to attract advertisers or to find people or businesses willing to sell the *Dispatch.* Howard had to hawk his paper in Town House Square himself. The publisher also walked five miles a day delivering copies to his handful of subscribers. His cantankerous printing press frequently malfunctioned, and, because of the lack of sufficient type, Howard and Lee had to take pen in hand and fill in missing letters in every paper that came off the press.

By Christmas the two men were subsisting on beans, popcorn balls, squash pie, crackers, and coffee. Desperate, they published an appeal in the *Dispatch* for the opportunity to "renew acquaintance with a piece of roast beef or to look, once more, a chicken in the face."

Nevertheless, Arthur Howard met every challenge with a combination of courage and creativity. He traded free advertising space in the *Dispatch,* along with the complimentary tickets sent to the paper by local theatres, to his landlords for board. He sometimes printed the *Dispatch* on free wrapping paper collected from local butcher shops and grocery stores. Howard even sold his treasured Abraham Lincoln letter to keep his paper going.

When the Rockefellers' Standard Oil Company was viciously attacked in the *Salem Evening News,* Howard, who knew one of the Rockefeller sons from his school days in New York, printed a rebuttal in the *Dispatch.* Standard Oil ordered two thousand extra copies of that day's paper, thereby providing the publisher with desperately needed capital.

Howard's pluck and determination eventually gained him the respect of a group of reform-minded citizens. Merchants George Day and Bill Sanborn, Alderman "Link" Allen, and Herman Curtis saw a potential ally in Arthur Howard and his *Dispatch.* They would soon draw Howard into the world of reform politics.

From his new friends Howard learned that Salem was run by a number of cliques dominated by the likes of Joe Peterson, a contractor by profession and a former mayor of Salem; the McSweeney brothers; Alderman Mike Doyle; and on-again, off-again mayor John "Silk Hat" Hurley. These men ruled through intimidation and patronage and feared only Robin Damon, the all-powerful publisher of the *Salem Evening News.*

Arthur Howard feared no one. Gradually, blistering editorials and political exposés began crowding literary items off the pages of his *Dispatch*. In an article entitled "Both Ends and the Middle," Howard described how the McSweeney clan had gained control of the city liquor license permit process and were using it illegally to their own financial advantage.

Another issue of the paper carried an account of how Alderman Doyle had spent the taxpayers' money to provide a sewer hookup for the Salem Theatre and had been rewarded with jobs at the theatre for himself and a nephew at eyebrow-raising salaries. Howard attacked another well-connected citizen for using his influence to sell the city a parcel of land on Highland Avenue at a vastly inflated price for a new high school building.

Howard's unceasing calls for reform made him many new friends but little money. Small businessmen eager to advertise in the *Dispatch* often received threatening calls or visits from Robin Damon. Nevertheless, Howard pressed on. In a *Dispatch* editorial in early February 1909 the publisher noted that in the upcoming December election, "From Ward 1 to Ward 6 there is going to be a housecleaning. Reform with a capital R will sweep this town from end to end."

Two months later Arthur Howard, a resident of Salem for only six months, announced his candidacy for mayor of Salem. The publisher would have plenty of competition in his quest for the city's executive office. The field would ultimately include incumbent mayor Hurley, reform candidates Samuel Goodhue and Robert Pollock, and political insider William McSweeney.

Arthur Howard's candidacy was considered a long shot by most, but his enemies weren't taking any chances. During the campaign private detectives were sent to New York to investigate Howard's background. Someone stole or opened and read more than three hundred pieces of his mail. Rocks were thrown through the windows of both the boarding house where Arthur lived and his *Dispatch* office.

The intimidation finally got to Ralph Lee, Howard's loyal

printer. Lee departed Salem and the *Dispatch* for the safer confines of the U.S. Army. Howard eventually found a new printer, and in the summer of 1909 he started a second paper, the *Gazette.* Now he could scream, in huge Hearstian headlines, that two of the three newspapers in Salem supported his candidacy for mayor.

On July 10, Alderman Mike Doyle, furious over an article that had appeared in the *Dispatch,* filed a libel suit against its publisher. Howard refused offers of bail money and went to jail in the hopes of garnering sympathy votes. Some of Howard's most devastating attacks on corrupt Salem bosses, printed under the title MORE NEWS FROM [CELL] 45 were based on information gleaned from fellow prisoners.

The publisher spent three days in the Salem jail before an attack of rheumatism forced him to post bail. Shortly after his release, Arthur was again sued for libel, this time by *Salem Evening News* publisher Robin Damon. Howard's bail was posted by Daniel Hegarty, a liquor dealer and a sworn enemy of Robin Damon.

When the libel case was called in September, Howard was unavailable. The *Dispatch* publisher was in an out-of-town hospital recovering from a severe beating administered by William McSweeney's brother, Parker. The abuse was taking a terrible toll on Arthur's health. In the weeks before the December election he was living on quinine and water and weighed barely one hundred pounds. He could hardly speak above a whisper.

The scene in front of city hall on election night, December 14, 1909, was the wildest the city had ever witnessed. Supporters of the candidates jammed Washington Street, where they waved banners, exchanged banter and bets, and sang their respective campaign fight songs. Howard's backers were as vocal as any, even though their man was considered a three-to-one long shot going into the election.

Voter turnout was the largest ever for a Salem municipal election up to that time, with over 90 percent of eligible voters casting ballots. When the polls were closed and the votes were tallied, the new mayor of Salem, by a margin of 280 votes, was the remarkable Arthur Howard.

Arthur's supporters went crazy. They hired a band, commandeered automobiles, and abducted Howard from his office where he was putting together the election-day edition of the *Dispatch*. After a brief speech by a campaign manager (Howard couldn't talk), the victor was led on a boisterous celebratory tour of Salem neighborhoods.

The two-hour parade finally ended at the Salem train station. Howard offered a few whispered remarks before boarding the 10:30 train to Boston. From there Arthur would catch a connecting train to New York, where his father lay dying.

For Arthur Howard, winning that election was the "proudest moment" of his life. The sentiments of his enemies were probably best summed up in the lead paragraph of a *Salem Evening News* story that appeared the day after the election:

> If a fleet of hostile aeroplanes should come sailing over Salem and drop a couple of tons of dynamite down into Town House Square, the explosions wouldn't create any greater surprise and consternation than the results of yesterday's municipal election.

The Salem fire

The conflagration started with an explosion in Korn Leather Company at the corner of Boston and Bridge Streets just before 2:00 P.M. on June 25, 1914. The first newspaper account appeared in the *Salem Evening News* just a few hours later. That story included a report that twenty female employees of the Korn and Creedon leather factories had died. Mercifully, the rumor was unfounded.

The paper's headline the following day shouted CONFLA-GRATION LOSS ESTIMATED $10,000,000, and the eleven-line sub-heading that followed provided some of the details. The fire left in its wake a crescent-shaped path of destruction measuring a mile and a half long and half a mile wide. The fire, which start-ed in Blubber Hollow and was finally arrested just west of Derby Wharf, burned around the Chestnut Street and Essex Street neighborhoods but leveled much of South Salem and all of the Point area. "Scores of factory buildings and hundreds of houses" were reduced to piles of rubble. Amazingly only six people died.

Among the 1,800 buildings that burned were a fire station at Harbor and Lafayette Streets and a nearby orphanage that housed one hundred children and twenty-five nuns. The Naumkeag Mills on Salem Harbor, the city's largest employer, was leveled, as were nearly four hundred other businesses. The first to reopen, according to the *Salem Evening News,* was Emile Frazier's barber shop. Two days after his Boston Street building burned to the ground, Frazier was back cutting hair in a tent close by his permanent location.

Late in the day on June 25 the flames engulfed the National Fireworks building on New Derby Street. The impromptu dis-play that followed, a *Salem Evening News* reporter noted, was "a spectacular sight" and sent spectators scrambling for safety. Another exciting spectacle was a blazing scow that broke loose from a wharf on the South River and floated into the harbor.

Early newspaper reports estimated that as many as 15,000 people were left homeless as a result of the fire. These included seventeen firefighters and, unbelievably, every single one of the three hundred or more members of Local 1210 of the carpenters' union. The post office on Washington Street handled three thou-sand change-of-address forms in a single day. Postal workers were also swamped with thousands of Salem fire souvenir postcards, which appeared on the market just two days after the conflagra-tion.

The disaster brought out both the best and the worst in

people. Some of the true heroes, or heroines, were to be found at the telephone office on Norman Street. The switchboard operators who were on duty when the fire erupted stayed at their posts even when the fire got so close to their building that the windows became too hot to touch. When the electric lights and the auxiliary gas lamps went out, the women continued to work by lantern light. They and the other operators who voluntarily came in to work handled thousands of calls on the day of the fire.

Mr. and Mrs. Alphonse Soucy of Danvers, who had ten children of their own, opened their home to thirty-six residents of Salem's Point neighborhood, which had been "shorn of every living thing." A few days after the fire, a *Salem Evening News* reporter noted that Mrs. Soucy appeared to be "completely worn out."

Beverly Farms summer resident Henry Clay Frick was one of the first to come to the aid of the fire victims. The industrial baron donated $25,000 to the relief effort and made his automobiles available for transportation in the days following the fire. Mrs. Frick and her daughter Helen personally made deliveries of needed goods and transported people to the temporary camps set up at the Salem Willows, Bertram Field, and Forest River Park. Helen also opened her summer camp in Wenham to a group of mothers and their children who had lost their homes.

Crime control was an important issue in the week following the conflagration. The burned-out district of the city was placed under martial law, and militiamen had orders to shoot looters on sight. Many cases were reported of citizens falsely claiming to be fire victims in order to obtain free clothing, food, and furniture. Two such con men were caught in the act a few days after the fire and were immediately sentenced to a few months in the house of correction.

Career criminals flocked to Salem looking to take advantage of the confusion. One of the country's most infamous crooks, Harry Martin, was apprehended while "helping out" at a relief center. Police were also eagerly looking to collar other well-known thugs, including a "rogue of international infamy" who had been spotted in the city.

The peacekeeping militia didn't always live up to its name. One militiaman refused to believe that Director of Public Works Patrick Kelley, who was in charge of strategic dynamiting efforts during the fire, was actually a public official and proceeded to disable Kelley's automobile by slashing one of his tires.

One of the more painful and bizarre stories relating to the Salem fire involved the McNamara family. The McNamaras' residence at 21 Green Street was destroyed by the blaze, and the evening of the fire Mrs. McNamara, her two children, and her mother-in-law were driving to Swampscott to temporary shelter. On the way their automobile collided with another vehicle. The McNamara family members were thrown from their car and badly shaken up. The following day Mr. McNamara was struck on Lafayette Street by an automobile carrying nurses bound for the relief station at the Salem Armory. Happily, all survived.

Henry Miller and *The Black Cat*

The May 1919 issue of *The Black Cat*, a mystery magazine published by the Shortstory Publishing Company of Salem, carried a review of Carl Clausen's story "The Unbidden Guest" signed by Henry V. Miller—the same Henry Miller who would later pen the controversial *Tropic of Cancer* and *Tropic of Capricorn.*

For Miller it was the first time he saw his name in print. The budding author quickly became the periodical's top reviewer. He earned a whopping fifteen dollars for the five critical essays he contributed to *The Black Cat* before the magazine stopped carrying reviews in November 1919.

Caroline Emmerton and
The House of Seven Gables

❧

"Her days were filled with service to her fellowman, her heart and her purse were ever open to every call or need." So ended the obituary of Caroline Emmerton, "one of Salem's best-known and beloved citizens," in the March 17, 1942, *Salem Evening News.* Emmerton was born in 1866 into a Salem family long known for its philanthropic work. Her grandfather, the wealthy merchant John Bertram, founded Salem Hospital and a home for aged men. His family donated his Essex Street mansion to the city of Salem to serve as a public library after his death in 1880.

Caroline began her public service career when she was in her late twenties. She served on the boards of many local social service agencies, including the Seaman's Widow and Orphan Society and the Plummer Home for Boys. She also helped organize a series of baby-weighing stations, or clinics, that provided health care for Salem's immigrant population.

In 1907 Caroline spearheaded the drive to open a settlement house in Salem to serve the city's growing immigrant population. The following year she bought the House of Seven Gables on Turner Street and set out to restore it as a museum. She later acquired the seventeenth-century Hooper-Hathaway and Retire Becket Houses and had them moved to the Gables grounds.

Proceeds from the admissions charged at the new museum helped to support settlement programs held in adjacent Turner Hall. Newcomers to Salem could take courses in manual training, citizenship, nursing, and sewing. Members of the House of Seven Gables Settlement's Mothers Club were occasionally treated to a long drive in the country in Ms. Emmerton's chauffer-driven limousine.

To raise funds for the operation of the settlement house, Emmerton organized the Salem Pageant in 1913. For four days in June a cast of over a thousand, including two complete military regiments and members of at least ten local historic societies, re-created episodes from Salem history on the grounds of the Kernwood estate in Salem, now the Kernwood Country Club. Accompanying the actors was a 150-member chorus.

The *Salem Evening News* called the Salem Pageant "the greatest historical spectacle ever held in Salem." Unfortunately, the event raised only a few thousand dollars.

Ms. Emmerton employed a professional staff at the House of Seven Gables but personally oversaw every facet of the operation. Former guides recalled that she would sit in Judge Pyncheon's chair in the dining room and listen to the information being given out by the guides. Any erroneous statement was corrected on the spot, right in front of the visitors.

While the House of Seven Gables museum and settlement were the major focus of her life (she left them the bulk of her estate), Caroline was also heavily committed to the Salem Fraternity boys club. She served as a director in the 1920s and 1930s and helped the organization buy a camp in Rowley. Each summer Caroline spent a few weeks at the camp teaching courses and counseling the youngsters.

The Yankee priest

One of the characteristics that endeared Caroline Emmerton to local citizens was the personal interest she took in many of the youngsters who attended the House of Seven Gables Settlement House or the Salem Fraternity. One of her favorite protégés was Eddie Murphy. Eddie grew up on Curtis Street just a stone's throw from the settlement house.

Ms. Emmerton recognized Eddie's artistic inclinations and talent and took him on trips to Boston to art museums, concerts, and plays. When the youngster won a scholarship from the Archdiocese of Boston to attend the Jesuit high school of his choosing, Ms. Emmerton told Eddie that he wouldn't be needing it. Unbeknownst to the Murphy family, she had made other arrangements for Eddie to pursue his education. But Eddie, inspired by Father Timothy Murphy at St. Mary's Church, had made up his mind to enroll at Epiphany College in Baltimore, Maryland, in preparation for the priesthood.

Caroline Emmerton would soon have plenty of reason to be proud of her former protégé. Father Edward Murphy became famous for his work with the African-American community in New Orleans and as the author of a number of religious novels, including the first Catholic best-seller, *The Scarlet Lily.* He later penned a popular autobiography entitled *The Yankee Priest.*

More Gables stories

During the 1970s the House of Seven Gables Settlement hosted an active evening program for neighborhood teenagers. The teens took classes, played basketball in the upstairs gymnasium at the settlement's Emmerton Hall, or just hung out. There were also occasional field trips.

One overnight trip to Salisbury Beach Campground in 1975 turned out to be a particularly sleepless one for the teen program staff and other adults who had been recruited to act as chaperones. Because the weather report was not promising, a decision was made the next morning to return home as soon as possible.

As the adults struck the tents and packed up the equipment, a small group of teens got into a debate about whether the glowing orb in the generally overcast sky was the sun or the moon. As voices were raised and the opinions hardened, the combatants appealed to a higher authority, teen program director Bob Leonard, for the correct answer.

"Bob," one of the teens asked pointing to the softly glowing disk, "is that the sun or the moon?"

The mischievous Leonard, after a quick glance at the sky, shrugged his shoulders and replied, "I don't know. I'm not from around here."

❦

After working for thirty years at the House of Seven Gables, Eddie Luzinski was retiring as superintendent of property.

The Salem Evening News ran a front-page story about his career and memories of his years at this popular house museum on Salem Harbor. A photograph of Eddie seated in a wrought-iron chair in the Gables garden was to accompany the story.

In the first issues to come off the press, many of which reached the reading public, the photograph of Eddie was inadvertently switched with another that was also to appear on the front page. The photograph that accompanied the caption telling of Eddie Luzinski's retirement from the House of Seven Gables was a picture of a man being led off in handcuffs by two detectives.

Putt's Club

❦

For more than a quarter of a century the Putnam Club, or "Putt's Club," as it was more commonly known, was a fixture on the Salem cultural scene. The club was started and run by Alfred Putnam of Summer Street, who willingly accepted the mantle of benevolent dictator and had no rules or bylaws.

Membership was by invitation only. Among the club members were historian and author James Duncan Phillips; Parker Brothers game company founder George S. Parker; and Ralph Cowan Browne, the inventor of the magnetic mine that was instrumental in winning World War I.

Putt's Clubbers met monthly at the homes of various members to eat and listen to a paper prepared by the host. Topics might include a biographical sketch of Albert Schweitzer or Salem's famed architect and carver Samuel McIntire. Other lecture themes included bullfighting, bird life in Florida, gambling, James Joyce's *Ulysses,* Mary Shelley's *Frankenstein,* and Salem in the War of 1812.

Meetings were occasionally held in settings more exotic than a member's drawing room. Alfred Putnam remembered reading his paper in front of a campfire "on the windswept fields of [Judge Alden White's] Wood Chuck Farm in Danvers by the light of a flickering lantern."

The club's gatherings were occasionally enhanced by the presence of guests invited by one of the members. The most famous guest was the sitting Vice President of the United States, Calvin Coolidge. "Silent Cal" was, as usual, difficult to engage in conversation. When a member tried to elicit some feedback from Coolidge about the Federal Reserve System, the vice president replied, "It seems to work."

End of discussion.

Salem builds a hotel

◆

At a Salem Rotary Club meeting on May 27, 1921, Salem Laundry owner George Hooper took the floor to address an issue of paramount importance to Salem.

Hooper reminded his fellow Rotarians that hundreds of

businessmen visited Salem each month, and that tourists were coming in ever-increasing numbers. The problem, he noted, was that there was no place in Salem for them to stay. The lack of a sizable modern hotel, like those being built in cities across the country, was hurting Salem's economy and reflected badly on the city.

Hooper's comments were well received by club members, who promptly appointed him and Frank Poor of the Hygrade Lamp Company as a committee of two to explore the feasibility of building a new hotel in Salem. A few months later George Hooper was elected president of the Salem Chamber of Commerce, which then became the hub for future hotel-related activities.

Throughout 1922 and 1923, the Chamber of Commerce column in the *Salem Evening News* frequently stressed the need for a new hotel in Salem. In the winter of 1922, a steering committee began developing plans to meet that need, and the work of that committee led to the organization of the Salem Hotel Corporation (incorporated on August 27, 1923). Included on the corporation's fifty-two-member executive committee were Hooper, Poor, Chamber of Commerce Secretary Roscoe Goddard, George Parker of Parker Brothers, and Henry Benson of the Naumkeag Steam Cotton Company.

A decision was made to begin fund-raising for the new hotel in July 1923. Another 175 volunteer businessmen were recruited to help the executive committee in the effort. The Hockenbury Company of Harrisburg, Pennsylvania, which specialized in fund-raising for community hotels, was retained to coordinate the stock subscription campaign. The sales corps was divided into sixteen teams and four divisions. Its members underwent intensive training in the selling of stock by Hockenbury personnel.

The week-long stock subscription drive kicked off with a rally at Ames Hall in the Salem YMCA on July 16, 1923. Motivational speeches were followed by the singing of popular

The proprietors of the Hawthorne Hotel had some creative ideas about how to deal with the loss of business resulting from the Great Depression.

songs—including "Bananas" and "My Old Kentucky Home"—whose lyrics had been rewritten to reflect the task at hand. Music was provided by the Salem Rotary Club band.

The Chamber of Commerce office on Washington Street served as headquarters for the subscription campaign. Daily luncheon meetings were held in Ames Hall to review sales results. The updated totals were posted on a huge billboard in Town House Square.

Quarter-page ads in the *Salem Evening News* reminded the local citizenry that buying stock in the new hotel was their "civic duty." The Salem Hotel Corporation published its own "Ho! Tell!—A Daily Journal of Stock-Sales Dope" each day during the subscription drive.

More than half of the Salem Hotel Corporation's goal of $500,000 was met on the first day. By the end of the campaign, over a thousand individuals and businesses, including every member of the Salem Rotary Club, had purchased at least one share of stock in the hotel. The less affluent employees of the Salem Laundry Company and other businesses pooled smaller amounts of money to buy a group share.

The drive officially ended on July 24. Bill Leslie filled in the final total—$527,000—on the Town House Square billboard as the assembled campaign workers sang and cheered.

With more than two-thirds of the $750,000 needed to build the hotel in hand, the Salem Hotel Corporation went to work. A site adjacent to the Salem Common was chosen over another on the corner of Front and Central Streets opposite the police station. Land acquisition was completed by January 1924. The Salem Marine Society even agreed to sell its Franklin Building and let it be razed to make way for the hotel.

Contractors were hired, including the local construction firm of Pitman and Brown and architect Phillip Horton Smith of Smith and Walker in Boston. The American Hotel Company was chosen to manage the new hostelry.

Construction began in June 1924, and the project took a year to complete. A month before the hotel was to open, a decision was made to raise an additional $90,000 to pay for an expanded main ballroom and to reduce the size of the mortgage. Those funds were raised in just a few days again using the Hockenbury system.

The spirit of community cooperation was contagious. Hotel stock salesmen agreed to help raise $10,000 for the Hawthorne Memorial Association, which was in the process of buying deceased sculptor Bela Lyon Pratt's statue of Salem author Nathaniel Hawthorne. The sculpture was moved from Boston to a location just a few yards from the new hotel and dedicated in December 1925.

The 150-room colonial revival Hawthorne Hotel, named for the city's most famous native son, opened on July 23, 1925. The festivities lasted three days. Separate banquets were held for the contractors and shareholders, and a public open house attracted as many as 2,500 people in a single day. A community parade and flag-raising by Governor Alvin Fuller preceded the grand opening banquet on July 25.

The occasion was one of tremendous civic pride for local residents. The city's success, George Hooper noted, was proof that "we can do anything we want to by getting together and working."

The proprietors of the Hawthorne Hotel had some creative ideas about how to deal with the loss of business resulting from the Great Depression. The hotel owners had a fourteen-foot skiff mounted on the chassis of an automobile and rigged it with a single sail. The land yacht, under the command of Clarence Bohanon, and powered by the car's engine, then "set sail" in 1931 for ports throughout New England to distribute Salem tourist information.

Salem Trade

Since instituting its football program in 1890, Salem High School has had many memorable teams and moments. The school's 1931 squad went through an entire ten-game regular season without giving up a single point. The 1925 team, arguably the program's greatest ever, capped off an undefeated 14-0-1 season with a 44-7 thrashing of Leon High of Tallahassee, Florida.

Salem High even sent a football player to the Hall of Fame in Canton, Ohio. Wayne Millner (class of 1929) played end for the University of Notre Dame and the Washington Redskins and was inducted into the Hall of Fame in 1968.

And then there was Salem Trade. The Trade squad was not known for its winning ways (in fact, it often lost by design), but for somehow managing to play a full schedule for three years in the 1920s without its secret being discovered.

There was no Salem Trade School in Salem. Most locals assumed the team's players went to the vocational school on Broad Street. A few did, but many of them attended no school at all. Much of the squad was composed of high school dropouts. Half of the players were over twenty-one years old.

Harold Burgess, the team's quarterback and coach, created the Trade squad. He scheduled mostly away games to reduce the chances that the team would be found out. Salem Trade traveled as far away as Hingham on the South Shore. Because they weren't very good, the Trade squad had no trouble finding opponents.

The Salem Trade mailing address was the Salem Fraternity boys' club on Central Street. Uniforms and equipment came from various sources. The jerseys were Salem High rejects. Prisoners at the local jail made the helmets.

The Trade squad managed to escape detection for three years despite the huge crowds—as many as three thousand fans—that attended their rare home games on Salem Common. But the bubble finally burst a few games into the 1928 season after a 20-0 loss to Revere. Someone "dropped a dime" on the squad, and the story ran on the front page of the *Boston Globe.*

A number of team members pointed an accusing finger at Harold Burgess. The player-coach had performed poorly in the game and had been forced to walk home. But Burgess never confessed. According to historian Bob Cahill, he later moved to Texas and organized the fictional Burgess High School football squad. The "school," Cahill noted, was a supermarket.

Pioneer Village

&

America's first living history museum is not Colonial Williamsburg or Plimouth Plantation but Salem's own Pioneer Village.

In 1929 the city of Salem set out to re-create Salem as it would have appeared at the time of John Winthrop's arrival in 1630. The project was part of Salem's contribution to the Massachusetts Tercentenary celebration in 1930. Overseeing the work was George Francis Dow. The noted antiquarian-architect insisted whenever possible that seventeenth-century materials and construction methods be utilized.

The spot chosen for the eleven-acre village was a harborfront site in Forest River Park. The village featured various types of early colonial dwellings including dugouts, wigwams, and thatched-roof cottages. The centerpiece was a re-creation of the "fayre house" that had been built for Governor John Endicott after his arrival in 1628.

Five thousand plants, trees, and shrubs representing species known to have grown in the Salem area in 1630 added an air of authenticity. So did the saw pit, saltworks, and blacksmith shop.

The city's newest historic attraction even boasted a replica of John Winthrop's ship *Arbella.*

Pioneer Village opened in June 1930 and remained a popular tourist destination well into the 1950s. Among the tens of thousands of visitors were President Calvin Coolidge and actress Bette Davis. For a variety of reasons the site gradually deteriorated in the 1960s and 1970s. Fires, vandalism, and neglect took their toll. Finally, in 1985, the City of Salem Park Commission voted to raze the village.

A year later, however, the commission was signing a contract with Pioneer Village Associates, headed by Peter LaChapelle of the Salem Maritime National Historic Site and David Goss of the House of Seven Gables, who agreed to restore and manage the once-popular site. Their goal was to establish seventeenth-century authenticity whenever finances would allow. In all, the restoration team raised approximately $200,000.

In the ensuing few years Goss, LaChapelle, and other museum professionals and volunteers worked to restore Pioneer Village to its former glory. They cleared and burned acres of brush, planted herb gardens, and, with the help of retired carpenter and volunteer extraordinaire Bob Leblanc, they rebuilt every structure in the village. The wigwam and roofs of the cottages were thatched by two brothers from Ireland. Enhancing the visitor's experience were specially bred animals from Plimouth Plantation.

Although the village was open on a full-time basis by the 1988 tourist season, the grand reopening of Pioneer Village was held in June 1990. The following year Goss and LaChappelle won the American Society of Travel Writers' prestigious Phoenix Award for their roles in the restoration effort.

Monopoly saves the day

The year was 1933 and Parker Brothers, the fifty-year-old Salem game company, was in serious financial trouble. Despite fresh leadership, new streamlined production methods, and a catalog of games that included the popular Rook, Ping-Pong, and Pastime Puzzles, sales and profits had fallen off dramatically. The company desperately needed a winner.

Enter Charles Darrow, an underemployed engineer from Germantown, Pennsylvania. A tinker by nature, Darrow had invented a board game that drew on his fond memories of childhood visits to Atlantic City on the New Jersey coast. He called the game Monopoly.

Darrow's friends and neighbors so enjoyed playing Monopoly that the inventor began producing sets by hand and selling them. Eventually the demand grew to the point where Darrow had to have the games factory-produced.

Charles Darrow felt Monopoly could be his ticket out of poverty. In 1934 he approached Parker Brothers. Company executives played Monopoly, and although they personally enjoyed the game, they felt it had "52 fundamental playing errors." The game took too long, they said, and was too complicated.

Despite the rejection, Darrow still believed in Monopoly. Returning home he ordered five thousand copies of the game and sold them all to the prestigious Wanamakers department store in Philadelphia. The news of that transaction caught the attention of Parker Brothers executives. A new round of discussions between the company and Charles Darrow led to a royalty deal that made Darrow a wealthy man.

For most of 1935 and 1936 Monopoly kept the Salem company afloat. The firm had enjoyed many successes since George Parker started the business fifty years earlier, but never anything approaching the sales of its newest offering. An outside company had to be brought in to handle the overwhelming volume of orders.

But the firm almost shot itself in the foot again. In December 1936 George Parker issued an order to cease production of Monopoly. His feeling was that like every board game, it had run its course. But George got lucky. A sudden upturn in orders for Monopoly prompted him to rethink his decision.

Monopoly subsequently went on to become what the company describes as "the world's most popular board game and the best-selling copyrighted game in history."

Frank Weston Benson

❧

"Oh no, you won't. I'll not have two sons be painters. I can only support one artist."

So spoke George Benson, a prosperous Salem cotton merchant to his son John. The youngster had simply asked to be allowed to join his brother Frank at art school.

George needn't have worried about supporting Frank. Soon after his return from Académie Julian in Paris in 1885, the young artist was hired to teach antique painting at the Museum School at the Museum of Fine Arts in Boston. He would remain at the school until 1931.

At the same time Frank also joined his friend Edmund Tarbell in a Boston studio and embarked on what would be a wildly successful career as a painter of portraits *en plein air* and hunting and fishing scenes. In 1914 he was called the "nation's most medaled painter" by the *Boston Transcript*.

With the critical acclaim came wealth. According to a biographical sketch written by Frank's granddaughter, Benson's income from the sale of etchings alone in the decade of the 1920s was $80,000 a year. In the month of January 1929 Frank sold enough paintings and etchings to earn him an eye-popping $68,000. Benson owned a farm on North Haven Island in Maine and a rambling Greek revival house on Salem's elegant Chestnut Street.

Frank's younger brother, John, incidentally, also did well. Deprived of the opportunity to attend art school, he studied architecture at the Beaux Arts in Paris and went on to a long and successful career as an architect in New York. Later in life John began dabbling in art and established a reputation as a capable marine painter.

The Paramount

One of the saddest moments in the lives of Salem residents of recent decades was the closing of the Paramount Theatre in 1970.

The Paramount was a fixture in downtown Salem for forty years. The theatre was one of a series of venues built by the Salem Realty Company in partnership with Paramount Publix Corporation. The 2,200-seat facility cost approximately $1 million to construct and could proudly claim the distinction of being the first theater in the nation designed exclusively for "talkies."

The Paramount, which billed itself as "The North Shore's Greatest Amusement Institution," was truly a showcase. The entrance was located at 180 Essex Street, but the theater itself sat on a rear lot adjacent to Church Street. Moviegoers passed through the front entrance and proceeded toward the lobby down a long hallway lined with posters advertising coming attractions. The hallway passed under the New Essex House, a famous Salem residential hotel.

The hallway, lobby, and theater were all decorated in the French Renaissance style. The furniture was Louis XV, the color scheme a blend of ivory, blue, coral green, and gold. The seats were upholstered in green patterned mohair. The walls inside the theater were adorned with eight enormous murals "in the style of Fragonard, Watteau, and Boucher."

Everything about the Paramount bespoke elegance. Phyllis Luzinski of Salem, recalling her first trip to the theater when she was eight or nine years old, said, "I was stunned by the ladies' room. It had a separate waiting room with fancy sofas and a dressing table with probably eight seats. I had never seen anything like it."

The Paramount's crack usher corps helped set the tone for the theater. "Most of the ushers were tall, good-looking young men, the type the young women swooned over," remembered Ed Zielinski. "They wore red-and-black uniforms trimmed with gold braids and caps. They were an impressive sight."

The Paramount opened on April 19, 1930, with a kickoff parade through downtown Salem. The first showing of the first movie, *Honey,* starring Nancy Carroll, started at 10:00 A.M. and ran continuously until 6:00 P.M., alternating with Laurel and Hardy's *Below Zero.*

A special newsreel, *Historic Salem,* was screened at the official opening ceremony that evening. Some of the footage had been shot earlier in the day by Paramount Publix cameramen and rush-processed in Boston.

The week following the opening, April 21–26, was designated "Salem Paramount Week" in the city.

After the hoopla subsided, the theater settled down to routine business. The movie fare at the Paramount changed twice a week, on Sundays and Thursdays. Admission in the early days was thirty-five cents for adults, more for orchestra and loge seating after 6:00 P.M. Smoking was permitted in the upstairs balcony.

For a time, theater patrons received free transportation home on the local trolley system. Theatergoers only had to show the trolley conductor their theater ticket stub.

The Paramount's crack usher corps helped set the tone for the theater.

In addition to movies, the Paramount also offered a regular schedule of live performances by big-name stars. Former patrons would remember seeing Ted ("Is Everybody Happy?") Lewis and his orchestra, Louis Armstrong, and Chico Marx onstage. Dorothy Lamour and Alfred Hitchcock also appeared at the Paramount.

But the movies were still the main attraction. Some films and stars were decidedly more popular than others. "I saw *Gone with the Wind* three times at the Paramount," said Jean Jalbert. "Like many other young women, I went every time it came back. And I was dragged to the Paramount four times to see *A Song to Remember* by a friend who was madly in love with the star, Cornell Wilde."

One of the most significant cinematic events in the theater's history occurred in 1940 when the Paramount screened the world premiere of the 20th Century-Fox film *The House of the Seven Gables.* All proceeds from the showing were donated to the House of Seven Gables Settlement programs. Unfortunately for the public, the movie's star, Margaret Lindsey, was a no-show at the premiere.

Another attraction at the Paramount was its celebrated organ. The 1,400-pipe, sixteen-ton instrument was one of just nine made by the Wurlitzer Company for theaters. The organ was mounted on an elevator platform, which rose up from the orchestra pit on cue. The organ was designed to provide music and special sound effects, from bird calls or a fire siren to a two-hundred-piece orchestra, for silent films.

But because the Paramount showed "talkies," its organ was used primarily for sing-alongs between movies at double features. As Frank Simpson, Tom Smith, or one of the other Paramount organists played, patrons would sing, "following the bouncing ball" as it worked its way along the lyrics projected on the screen.

The Paramount survived the Depression and World War II but began to decline in the 1950s. The mobility provided by the automobile and highways made theaters in Boston and other communities more accessible, thereby increasing competition. The gradual demise of Salem's once-bustling central business district in the early 1960s drew even more potential theatergoers away from the Paramount.

The Paramount died a quiet death in 1970 and was torn down in the spring and summer of 1971 to make way for a new indoor mall. The marvelous organ was sold to Charles French of Weston, who planned to use it as the centerpiece of a new museum.

His museum never materialized, however, and this last piece of Salem's grandest theater was sold to the Pizza and Pipes restaurant in Seattle, Washington, in 1974.

The Rialto

၆၅

Two seniors, a man and a woman, in the waiting room of a local dental office began reminiscing about downtown Salem in its retail heyday.

"There were Sears, Almy's, Webbers, and Empire for department stores," remembered the woman, "and the five-and-dimes. Plus Daniel Low's, the Salem Rubber Shop, and Ted Cole's Music Store."

"Don't forget Moustakis' Candy Store," chimed in the man, "and all the movie theaters. We had the Salem, the Paramount—"

"And the Rialto," interrupted the woman, "with the fur-lined seats." The two laughed.

The latter comment got the attention of a third, significantly younger waiting patient. "Salem had a movie theater with fur-lined seats?" he asked incredulously.

The seniors laughed. "No," said the woman. "What the phrase referred to was that no matter where you sat in the theater, at some point during the movie a rat was likely to brush up against your leg!"

Uncovering old homes

In the early 1960s Elizabeth Reardon of Salem and a few of her friends signed up for a ten-session course in colonial architecture offered by the Society for the Preservation of New England Antiquities (SPNEA).

At the conclusion of the third lecture, the students were given checklists of architectural features that are typical of seventeenth-century New England dwellings. Armed with her list, Libby Reardon revisited a small Victorian cottage at the corner of Liberty and Charter Streets that had caught her eye years earlier.

As she surveyed the exterior of the building, Reardon got excited. Despite the mansard roof and other Victorian features, she felt fairly sure that the house had been built before 1700.

Reardon arranged with city officials to allow her to tour the vacant house with Abbott Lowell Cummings, then assistant director of the SPNEA. Cummings had been dubious when Reardon had first called him about her possible discovery. "Young lady, if you have found a seventeenth-century house in Salem that I don't know about, I shall be very surprised," Cummings had told her.

One look at the interior framing of the dwelling was enough to convince Cummings that his skepticism had been unfounded. The structure, Cummings determined, had been built in the early 1660s.

Reardon and Cummings then repaired to Libby's Chestnut Street home where they celebrated their discovery over a glass of sherry and peanut butter sandwiches. The house, now named for its original owner Samuel Pickman, was eventually restored through the combined efforts of Historic Salem, Inc., and a private developer.

The SPNEA's architectural course would reap additional dividends when Reardon uncovered yet another seventeenth-century house on High Street in Salem. The SPNEA was able to acquire that dwelling, which was built for Eleazer Gedney in 1664, and now uses it to illustrate seventeenth-century construction techniques and architecture.

Bessie Monroe saves her house

❧

When the wrecking crew arrived at 2 Ash Street one morning in 1968 to begin demolishing Bessie Monroe's house, they were taken aback to find the elderly owner still there.

Bessie's home was one of dozens that was to be razed according to the Salem urban renewal plan that had been approved by state and federal agencies in 1967. Many preservationists had objected to the planned demolition of Monroe's home. The brick Ash Street house had been built in 1811 and was rare among buildings of the federal style because it was only two stories high.

The preservationists may have failed to save the house, but Bessie did not. She simply told the demolition crew that if the building came down it would be on top of her. She had no intentions of leaving. Not surprisingly, Bessie Monroe's home still stands on Ash Street.

The making of "The Witch City"

Despite its plethora of important historical events and architectural specimens and treasures, Salem has gradually become known to much of the outside world as the Witch City.

Many Salem businesses and institutions have encouraged this development over the years. One of the first commercial uses of the witch theme was made by Pettingells Fish Company, a mainstay business on Derby Wharf in the last quarter of the nineteenth century. Pettingells sold fish under eight separate brand names, one of which was Witch City.

The selling of Salem witch souvenirs was the brainchild of Daniel Low. The Essex Street jeweler produced the first witch spoon just in time for the two hundreth anniversary of the Salem witch trials in 1892, and in so doing he spawned a whole new industry. The popular spoons were followed by plates, pins, charms, and other souvenir items bearing a facsimile of a witch on a broom or some other witch motif.

Less successful was Parker Brothers' attempt to capitalize on the infamy of the Salem witch trials. The firm's Ye Witchcraft Game appeared on store shelves in 1889, but negative public reaction from what the company later described as "oversensitive Salemites" led Parker Brothers to remove the game from the market.

Not everyone was offended by the use of the witch theme or motif for nonhistoric purposes. In the 1893–1894 Salem City Directory, Mrs. Frank Stone advertised that her boarding house at 1 Sewall Street would henceforth be known as the Witch City House. In that same directory the Witch City Bottling Works was listed at 4-6 Sewall Street. By the turn of the century a popcorn works, a boat yard, a bicycle manufacturer, and an oil firm were also using the Witch City name.

The late nineteenth century also saw the rise of the

Witches, a fraternal organization that was a mainstay of political campaigns and election night victory parades. A *Salem Evening News* account of the celebration of General William Cogswell's election to Congress in 1888 noted that the "Salem Witches, 85 strong" marched in the parade and were accompanied by a "pretty little skye terrier" dressed in a witch's cloak and hat. The men also wore witch outfits and carried brooms in place of rifles.

The Salem High School sports teams also came to be known as the Witches. Two former Salem high school football standouts, Joe "Pep" Cornacchio and Louis Mroz, remembered the name coming into use in the late 1930s or early 1940s. Those dates coincide with the appearance of a witch on a broom on the cover of the Salem High School yearbook in 1939 and the renaming of the student annual *The Witch* the following year.

Witch City Drum Corps, sponsored by Salem VFW Post 1524, came into national prominence about this time. The corps's juniors won the national championship in 1938, bringing more attention to Salem's notoriety.

In the decade between 1935 and 1945, the city's first witch attractions appeared. The Goodell family opened the Old Witch Jail and Dungeon in their rambling home on Federal Street in 1935. The house contained many of the timbers of the jail and dungeon used during the witch trials of 1692. For a small admission fee tourists could visit a replica of the dungeon where convicted "witches" awaited their date on Gallows Hill, and they could view artifacts that supposedly had belonged to some of the unfortunate victims. The opening of the attraction was covered live on the radio on the Yankee Network and was broadcast around the world.

The Old Witch Jail and Dungeon drew tens of thousands of visitors before it was razed in 1956 to make way for the New England Telephone Company's new building. It would soon be joined by a second historic site with connections to the 1692 witch trials. In 1944 the city established Historic Salem, Inc., for the purpose of restoring the former home of witch trial judge

Jonathan Corwin. The only Salem building extant with connections to the witch trials opened to the public as the Witch House in 1948.

In the 1960s and 1970s a number of important Salem institutions adopted the Witch City theme. A witch on a broom was added to the masthead of the *Salem Evening News,* the region's preeminent daily paper, on April 2, 1962. The Salem Chamber of Commerce adopted a similar motif for its logo, and Salem Police Department cruisers and uniforms were adorned with an image of a witch in flight and the phrase "Witch City." The fire department followed suit in 1992.

Tourism brochures from the 1960s show that the twenty-two sites on the city's historic trail were marked by signs featuring the now-commonplace pointy-chinned hag on a broom, even though the Witch House and Gallows Hill were the only witch-related stops on the tour. The image of a witch also appeared prominently on signs posted at the main entryways to the city.

Salem's reputation as the Witch City would be solidified in the early 1970s. Two episodes of the popular television sitcom *Bewitched* were filmed in Salem and surrounding communities and aired nationally during Halloween week in 1970. Elizabeth Montgomery and the rest of the cast and crew of the show stayed at the Hawthorne Hotel. Mayor Samuel Zoll proclaimed the last week in October "Bewitched Week" in Salem.

In 1971 Laurie Cabot, a Salem resident and one of America's high-profile Wiccans, opened what would be the first of many witch shops in the city. There one could buy items related to the Wiccan religion, including potions, tarot cards, and books. The following year the Salem Witch Museum, which offered a multimedia presentation about the Salem witch trials, opened on Washington Square.

Other witch attractions and shops followed. Then in 1982 the city hosted its first "Haunted Happenings" Halloween festival featuring haunted houses, candlelight tours, costume parades and balls, and other activities appropriate to the season. The event has grown into one of the largest in New England and brings tens of thousands of visitors each year to what has truly become, at least at Halloween, the Witch City.

April fools

☙

Although it hardly ranked with Orson Welles's infamous "War of the Worlds" broadcast, Salem had its own media hoax on April 1, 1969.

The perpetrator was longtime North Shore journalist Howard Iverson, then a reporter for the *Salem Evening News*. According to a front-page article bearing Iverson's byline, the Pentagon was considering Salem's Riley Plaza as one of three sites for a "Playsafe anti-antiballistic system" facility. If the plan was approved, the article said, construction would begin "as soon as the area is cleared of cars abandoned during the February snowstorms."

Both President Richard M. Nixon and Salem Congressman William Bates were said to support the proposal. "I don't want to wake up some morning and find out that the Russians have taken over Riley Plaza," Bates was quoted as saying.

At the end of the column Iverson acknowledged that the story was an April Fool's prank. But many readers apparently never read that far. The following day's edition of the news carried a retraction and mentioned that many outraged citizens had called to express their opposition to the proposal.

The Salem Market

In 1816 John Derby and Benjamin Pickman, Jr., gave to the town a parcel of land between Essex and Front Streets that until recently had been the site of Elias Derby's mansion. The deed for the land stipulated that the town must build and maintain on the site a combination market house and town hall. It also mandated that a fish market be erected on the town hall flats and wharf just below the new market house. The town accepted the offer in May 1816. Construction commenced in August, and by mid-November the one-hundred-by-forty-foot structure was ready for occupancy. The official dedication of the new building was held the following July and was attended by President James Monroe.

The market portion of the two-and-a-half-story building opened for business shortly after the building was completed. The stalls on the first floor and in the basement had been auctioned off to purveyors of meats and provisions, as had the outdoor spaces for cart vendors.

The indoor retail activity in the market house lasted until the early 1930s, when the building was made into offices for the city government. The outdoor market at Derby Square continued to flourish for another forty years. Dozens of vendors of fish, meat, produce, flowers, and other provisions sold their goods out of collapsible wooden stalls on Friday evenings and Saturdays in the parking lot below the old market house. As many as ten thousand customers attended the market on a single Saturday.

Vendors paid two dollars a week for an eight-by-eight-foot space in Derby Square. They were responsible for building, assembling, and storing their own stalls, most of which consisted of sawhorses, planks, and canvas roofs. Sellers generally set up on Friday evening or by 7:00 A.M. on Saturday and sold until the legal closing time of 10:00 P.M.

Only vendors with permits could sell in the square, and health inspectors monitored the quality of the foodstuffs. John Cappuccio recalled that one inspector carried a bottle of ammonia, jokingly called "holy water" by the vendors, which he would spray on suspect meats or vegetables to prevent them from being sold.

The market attracted shoppers from all of southern Essex County. Businesses located in the commercial blocks adjacent to Derby Square and along Front Street also prospered. These included restaurants, taverns, pool halls, and wholesalers of produce and provisions.

Business was frequently conducted in French, Polish, Russian, Italian, and other languages. The names of many of the vendors, including Fahey, DeFrancesco, Sobicinski, and Letarte, reflected the ethnic diversity of the shoppers.

The colorful market scene in Derby Square lasted until the early 1970s, although it gradually declined after World War II as home refrigeration, competition from supermarkets, and other factors changed the buying habits of consumers.

In 1973 and 1974 the market area was bricked over by the Salem Redevelopment Authority. Open brick sheds known as the Salem Marketplace were constructed just south of Front Street for the vendors, but those who moved into them stayed but a short time. By the end of the decade, this charming piece of the Salem scene was history.

Further reading

Bentley, William. *The Diary of William Bentley.* The Essex Institute, 1905.

Felt, Joseph B. *Annals of Salem.* W. and S. B. Ives, 1827, 1828.

Ferguson, David L. *Cleopatra's Barge.* Little, Brown and Company, 1976.

Hurd, Hamilton. *History of Essex County, Massachusetts.* J. W. Lewis and Company, 1888.

King, Caroline Howard. *When I Lived in Salem.* Stephen Daye Press, 1937.

Mellow, James R. *Nathaniel Hawthorne In His Times.* Houghton Mifflin Company, 1980.

Moore, Margaret B. *The Salem World of Nathaniel Hawthorne.* University of Missouri Press, 1998.

Nissenbaum, Stephen, and Charles Boyer. *Salem Possessed.* Harvard University Press, 1974.

Payne, Ralph D. *The Ships and Sailors of Old Salem.* The Outing Publishing Company, 1908.

Perley, Sidney. *History of Salem* (3 volumes). Sidney Perley, 1924–1929.

Phillips, James Duncan. *Salem in the Seventeenth Century.* Houghton Mifflin Company, 1933.

Phillips, James Duncan. *Salem in the Eighteenth Century.* Houghton Mifflin Company, 1937.

Putnam, Eleanor. *Old Salem.* Houghton Mifflin and Company, 1886.

Robotti, Frances Diane. *Chronicles of Old Salem.* Newcomb and Gauss Company, 1948.

Starkey, Marion L. *The Devil in Massachusetts.* Alred A. Knopf, 1949.

Tagney, R. N. *A County in Revolution.* The Cricket Press, 1976.

Tharp, Louise Hall. *The Peabody Sisters of Salem.* Little, Brown and Company, 1950.

Watson, Thomas A. *Exploring Life.* D. Appleton and Company, 1926.

Winwar, Frances. *Puritan City.* National Travel Club, 1938.

Webber, C. H. and W. S. Nevins. *Old Naumkeag.* A. A. Smith and Company, 1877.